# ADONIS

# INCOGNITO

ADONIS, in Greek mythology, is the demigod of beauty and desire, and is a central figure in various mystery religions. His religion belonged to women: the dying of Adonis was fully developed in the circle of young girls around the poet Sappho from the island of Lesbos, about 600 BC, as revealed in a fragment of Sappho's surviving poetry.

Adonis is one of the most complex figures in classical times. He has had multiple roles, and there has been much scholarship over the centuries concerning his meaning and purpose in Greek religious beliefs. He is an annually-renewed, ever-youthful vegetation god, a life-death-rebirth deity whose nature is tied to the calendar. His name is often applied in modern times to handsome youths, of whom he is the archetype. Adonis is often referred to as the mortal god of Beauty.

From Wikepedia, the online encyclopedia

O, it's not what you **look like** when you're doin' what you're doin', it's what you're **doin'** when you're doin' what you look like you're doin'.

"Express Yourself",  Charles Wright and the Watts

103rd Street Rhythm Band

"Handsome is that handsome does."     Oliver Goldsmith

"The Captivity"

| CHAPTERS | | PAGE |
|---|---|---|

# CHAPTER ONE

## HALF & HALF

The tough-looking boy in front of me suddenly pulls a folding knife out of his pocket, opens it up and proceeds to throw it as hard as he can down into the ground within a couple of inches of my bare right toe. I jump back in surprise and alarm. I get a rude introduction to this move on the playground while wearing sandals at recess on my first day of kindergarten. After I jump back out of the way, the tough boy laughs and then explains what he is doing, using the moniker "mumbley pegs", which is the name of the game. The game apparently involves one guy throwing an opened-up pocket knife down hard so as to stick into the sandy ground close to someone else's foot, and then that person throws the same or his own pocket knife down into the ground close to the first guy's foot, and so on in a game of chicken to see who can get their knife closest to the other guy's foot.

I find this introduction to kindergarten very frightening for obvious reasons. It's bad enough that the farm kids seem to be so much bigger and rougher than I am. Now I have to worry about getting a knife stuck into my foot or leg. This is my first awareness of the 'town-gown' split in our village. It isn't really 'town-gown', but rather townie-farmer, and in this confrontation, it's the townies who are the more educated, effete ones.

Much later I get a fuller experience of this when I spend a week at the farm home of Loretta Leederhose, the baby sitter my mom hires to take care of us kids in my house, the one my sister, Elaine, calls "hush-push" for no particular reason that I can remember. During one of the periodic outbursts of rebellion by my sisters against Loretta, I discover on the mirror in our bathroom written in lipstick in big bold letters, "I hate hush-push." I have no idea why she hated Loretta at that moment.

Another time, I open the bathroom door to see Loretta just climbing out of the shower, and am amazed to see her full breasts and pubic hair. This is a revelation- she is a very beautiful and desirable young lady who has already fully matured physically.

Staying at Loretta's house is like going back into a more primitive time. There isn't even any running water in the house. I have to go outside to use an outhouse for a toilet and to the big well-pump to get water. They have a bunch of cows, and one morning I am out in the barnyard near the cows, which is kind of scary for me because these animals are so much bigger than I am. While I'm standing there, I am all of a sudden aware of a large splashing of water on the ground near me and I realize that one of the cows is taking a piss. It's like a blast from a fire hose and almost sprays on my legs. The cow is just standing there while this huge explosion of water pours down from her body onto the ground. No wonder the farmers all wear knee-high boots! This informs my later full understanding of the expression- "wetter than a double-cunted cow pissing on a flat rock."

Mostly during that week I am hanging with Loretta's younger brother George, who is a couple of years older than I am. One bright sunny, warm day I am struggling to lift up the hay bales from the field to George who is standing on the back edge of the horse-drawn wagon. George is working bareback, which shows off his muscular, tanned body. He picks up each bale I hand up to him and swings it around to the stacks starting from the front of the truck bed. This is very hard work for me, and makes me understand why George is so muscular.

The whole family works long hard hours for an entire 6-day week, but on Sunday, I am sitting around their parlor with them waiting for my mother to come and pick me up. The room is crowded with dull-colored over-stuffed furniture and has lace curtains on the windows. The family is all there along with aunts and cousins who have been invited to take part in the Sunday day off. Loretta's boyfriend is playing their upright piano. The boyfriend is a handsome young guy who seems like a city slicker, out of place in that farmhouse parlor. Loretta is beaming with pride at his looks and his playing, which is an extremely unskilled attempt to play like Liberace. I don't think of any such thing at the time because I don't know anything about it, but now I wonder if he was gay, although that doesn't seem very probable considering that Loretta is dating him, and I have already seen that she has the body of a full-grown woman.

Still, you cannot blame me for considering this possibility because it does seem that often the best-looking men and boys are gay. I know I'm getting way ahead of myself here, but decades later my wife is working in a doctor's office with a number of other women.  One day a 30ish, very well-dressed young male patient comes into the office who is extremely good-looking, plus he has the most impeccable manners, and is considerate, soft-spoken and polite, using highly educated language.  All of the women realize right away that the patient is gay, yet they are very favorably impressed with his looks and his manners and are all truly in awe. After he leaves, Dory makes the mock complaint to Sheila and the other women, "How come the gay professors, doctors and lawyers get all the best-looking guys, and all's we girls get is the sloppy leftovers?"

Fortunately, my kindergarten teacher soon puts a stop to mumbley pegs, so the boys revert to marbles, where the worst that can happen is that you literally lose your marbles. I feel intimidated by the farm kids because they are mostly bigger and stronger than I am, even though we are all in the same kindergarten, and I am especially afraid of the knife, because I imagine it being stuck into my foot or leg. Even though I have two older sisters and one younger one, I have not learned anything about girls outside the family and how I might relate to them, if at all.

Elaine and I have greatly amused ourselves by maintaining

separation from our parents and older siblings by using ourown secret coded language. Breakfast is called "bah-hah", and when we have pancakes for breakfast, we have "pah-hah for bah-hah." Mrs. Nicklas down the street is a woman that seems to be making a play for my father, at least in Mom's opinion, because Mrs. Nicklas keeps dreaming up home repair jobs that her husband is unable to do but my father is. We call her "Mih-hih-nih-hih," with the vowel sounding like the first "i" in the word "idiot", which is what we are acting like.

This secret language code is not that different from the one I learn and employ later as a teenager working a summer job in the cook tent at the carnival. The carnival travels around New York State with one-week engagements at a series of towns including Oswego, Corning, Elmira, Ithaca, and even down into Pennsylvania at Towanda. I am proud to be driving the company panel truck between venues. The carny language is designed to enable the carnival insiders to carry on conversations in front of the customers, who are called "marks", without the latter being able to understand what is being said. The code is extremely elementary. The speaker simply inserts an "iz," an "iza" or an "eeiza" into most of the words. So the speaker might say " This meeizark is really steiza stizupid." The carny listener, but hopefully not the mark, is able to mentally eliminate these extraneous syllables from what he is hearing.

Although I have been pals with my younger sister, and even sometimes with my next older one, who is three years older than I am, I am amazed when my older sisters get to be teenagers and boys actually ask them out. The girls in my kindergarten don't seem much different than my sisters, although Ida Mannington seems to exude a very unpleasant odor, which I associate for some reason with her panties when she is sitting on the kindergarten floor.

Even though I am a skinny kid intimidated by the other boys, the girls mostly seem to like me for some reason. My name Grady is made fun of by the boys, who sometimes chant "Grady is a lady." They don't do anything with my last name-Markell, so I am probably lucky that they don't say "Markell is hell." The pattern of my whole life is established this early- I am more comfortable around girls than boys. Even in kindergarten, I am already a ladies' man.

In first grade I learn the alphabet by picturing it as a suspension bridge like the GW bridge. From the left, I visualize the letters a-f as a gradual rising curve up to the high point of the bridge superstructure at the letters g, h & I, then sloping gradually downward along the 'bridge cables' in a long arc to the letters m, n, o & p at the bottom of the bridge center, then gradually upward again in a symmetrical arc rising up the bridge cable to the second tower high point around the letters s, t & u, then finally swooping again in a downward arc to the finish on the other shore with the letter 'z', symmetrical to the first arc up from a to h. I do not see this bridge on any of my school materials, it's just the way I picture the alphabet in my own mind.

I love to build skyscrapers on the living room floor using the standard block set in the form of lumber. You know what I am talking about- the unpainted wood blocks which are mostly rectangles of various sizes, but with some pieces in the shape of cylinders, curves and arches. I naturally set a pair of the largest blocks on the floor for the base of the structure, then another pair of the same size and shape across the first pair in the opposite direction, and so on up to the top using smaller and smaller blocks. I end up with a building reaching the ceiling of the living room. I have no diagrams to follow in making these structures, I just follow my own instincts, although, to be honest, I have loved pictures of the Empire State Building, so maybe I am trying to imitate that image.

My other favorite pastime as a young boy is to put together ever more difficult jig-saw puzzles, which greatly impresses my parents and grandparents because they would have trouble doing this nearly as quickly as I do, which causes them to think that I am very talented. However, in High School and college, none of the guidance counselors make any reference to architects or architecture, despite the fact that I am very proficient in math. This field is not even on their radar screen so I am unable to consider it because I am totally clueless that such a possible career even exists.

I have made friends with a neighbor girl- Callie Conway,who is also in my class of eight year olds.  We both live only two blocks from school, so frequently we walk to and from school together. On a warm spring day in May, we are walking back home from school, and, because it is such a nice day, we decide to detour a couple of blocks just for a change of scene. As we come around the corner onto Elm Street, we are accosted by an older girl- Susan Hotchfield, age about twelve, whom I know to be the daughter of the Presbyterian minister and whom I also know is an only child.  She is evidently more interested in me than in Callie, because she stands astride the sidewalk blocking my way, points a gun at me and orders  me,

"Take your pants down."

I am very reluctant to do this, because I don't want to show either girl my little boy's penis, of which I feel some shame because of my foreskin, which I feel is ugly.  I think the same thing later when I see foreskins on classical paintings and sculptures.  When I was an infant, my mother had me circumcized, but the operation was botched because she didn't have it done by a mohel but by a goy doctor in the hospital who didn't know what he was doing.  She didn't go to a mohel because she was hiding her Jewish background from everyone including our own family.  As a result, I have ended up with half a foreskin, symbolic of the fact that I am half-

Jewish. As a two or three-year old, my mother helps me take baths, during which she stresses to me,

"be sure to always clean under the skin or you will develop an unhealthy condition."

This manages to make me feel that there is something unpleasant and diseased about my penis. I'm sure that she feels guilty for not having taken me to a mohel to get circumcized so as to get a proper brit milah, which may have been only a faint echo of the guilt she probably felt for abandoning her Jewish family to marry a goy.

Decades later when I am in my forties and have eventually learned about my Jewish background, I finally correct this situation by getting a full circumcision, although I don't feel Jewish enough to go to a mohel plus I have no idea whether mohels perform circumcisions on adult males. My motivation in getting circumsized has nothing to do with being Jewish but rather with wanting to be more attractive to women. I also don't have a late bar mitzvah, as my older son has been urging me to do. He has married a Jewish girl, has learned about my, and therefore his, Jewish background and begins to follow some of the rituals, such as Friday night seder and sending his daughters to kinderschul. He considers himself to be Jewish, even though his own mother, Sheila, is not Jewish. He never has a late bar mitzvah himself, but both his daughters later have their Bat Mitzvahs.

I go to a urologist, and I get the operation with a local anesthetic. The doctor's nurse is a very attractive brunette who is close to my own age, and, while the doctor is performing the operation behind a curtain, which shields onlymy lower abdomen, I am carrying on a lively conversation with both of them.  I notice that, during the entire operation and conversation, her eyes are glued to what the doctor is doing. I feel so totally exposed while talking with a beautiful brunette, but it doesn't seem to constrain our conversation, which is very animated, if not flirtatious.  Probably I am less embarrassed with my exposure because it is in strictly a medical environment.  Maybe she is Susan Hotchfield now grown up, or at least doesn't have any brothers.  Still, I wonder why she is still so curious about the male member. Working for a urologist,  she must observe these types of operations frequently, although I don't really know how typical it is for an adult male to get a circumcision.

My mother is still hiding her Jewish background from everyone including our own family when I am on Onset beach at the age of thirteen, still clueless about this part of my origins.  I see this gorgeous dark-haired beauty standing on the beach in her skimpy bathing suit, and I think  "Wow, I would love to get acquainted with her!"  So I approach the beauty to try to meet her.  The first thing she says to me is,

"have you had your bar mitzvah?"

Say what? I have never heard these words before and haven't the faintest idea what she is talking about. In fact, it sounds as though she is speaking to me in a foreign language, and I look at her with a blank expression that tells her I'm not Jewish, so she turns away and that is that.

The irony of this situation is that the thing she wants to know, whether I am at least thirteen years old - old enough for her to pay attention to- is actually true- I had just had my thirteenth birthday a month earlier- as well as the fact that I am actually part Jewish, and with the most important part of that identification being that it is my mother who is Jewish. Even not knowing anything about the Jewish part of my background, had I at least known that a Bar Mitzvah is a ceremony for a boy who has reached the age of thirteen, I could at least have put her mind at ease on that score. In the actual situation though, I haven't the slightest clue about any of this so I make an out with that girl on the first pitch.

When Susan Hotchfield points her toy gun at me, I do as I am told- I don't want to get shot. I pull down my pants and underpants and silently stand there briefly, then pull them back up again. Though the whole event lasts less than a few seconds, it seems like an eternity. Callie is nearly as uncomfortable about this as I am, and as we continue walking home from school afterwards, neither of us says one word about it simply because the whole thing is so unbearably embarrassing. This is especially true since I have cowardly complied with Susan's demand when I should realize that the gun is only a toy so I needn't feel any compulsion about giving in to her order. If only I could feel more confident in my own physical strength, I would simply continue walking around her and pay no attention to her. Although she is a girl and I am aboy, she is much larger than I am. Still, a large part of why I feel so much chagrin is that I stupidly and meekly do as I am told.

It is evident from the point of view of hindsight that Susan is just curious about boys because she doesn't have any brothers. I imagine that she is pretty disappointed by what she sees.

It is at this time that I also start to have problems with male bullies. One of them is Callie's older brother Dave. He sometimes menaces me while I am walking to or from school with Callie. He stands in front of us with feet planted wide apart and says

" C'mon ahead, wimp, see if you can get by me."

I never challenge him because I am a foot shorter than he is and much more slightly built. I just wait for him to stop his strutting and posturing and move out of our way, and then I continue on to school with Callie, but I am afraid that eventually he will start hitting and hurting me.

The ultimate solution to my fear of Dave Conway and other bullies in school is to befriend a big dumb kid named John Kane, who for some reason is in our class, probably because he has been kept back one or two grades for stupidity and poor grades. John is unquestionably dumb, but he is very big and very friendly. I start hanging out with him after school, sometimes collecting bottles and cans for redemption, reading comics, or just hanging around. On occasion I try to give him a little tutoring, but this is pretty hopeless. When John is with me, no bully, including Dave, ever comes anywhere near us. The tactic works perfectly, just like with Tennessee Tuxedo and Chumley. It provides great peace of mind to have a free body guard.

I also have to deal with more subtle forms of bullying. My

next-door neighbor, Danny Crow, who is a couple of grades ahead of me, and who acts tough around me, comes from next door one day with baseball gloves and a ball and says,

"Let's play catch."

I have never played baseball to this point. I had listened to World Series games on the radio while working around the house with my father, but had never been to a professional game. I have seen the high school baseball team play a little, but I am unfamiliar with the equipment used in the game.

Danny is a stocky guy with a very short brush cut, and with a face that looks like a pit bull. Wearing fielder's gloves, we start playing catch along our property line. Danny throws very hard at very close range, as though he is pitching to a batter, and that causes my palm to sting painfully on each catch.

My impression is that Danny wants to hurt my hands as a way of showing that he is a tough guy while I am a wimp. And, unfortunately, I buy into that message. Right then and there I decide that I don't want to play baseball and get hurt like that all the time, and in fact this one little game of playing catch turns out to be one of the experiences that causes me to avoid contact team sports altogether.

I think now, I bet I should have been wearing a more heavily-padded glove, such as a catcher's mitt, since Danny was throwing very hard pitches at close range.  Maybe he had a much more heavily padded glove than I did.

It is only a year or two later when I find out that Susan Hotchfield is not the only girl who is curious about boys. By sixth grade, I have a real girlfriend, Julie Haverson, who is a good-looking blonde with a whole bevy of beautiful blonde older sisters. Having Julie as a girlfriend flatters my ego, not only because of her looks, but also because of all those beautiful sisters.  I feel that I've gotten myself hooked up with some kind  of royalty.  Julie and I are not old enough to do anything sexually, only perhaps a little smooching.

One afternoon after school, Julie and I are just hanging out with Ann Ward and Bobby Martin, two other friends in our grade. The school we attend has grades from kindergarten to 12th grade all within a single building in the center of town. Julie suggests

"Let's go and spy on the high school boys taking their showers."

The shower room is a two-story space below grade, with windows that are in the upper story space of the shower room, but which are at grade on the outside.  These windows have frosted glass, are normally closed, and can be opened only by hooking a long pole into the window clasps from the floor below. But this is a very warm spring day and Julie somehow knows that, on such a warm day, these windows may be open to provide ventilation to the shower room, and that we can stand right on the ground outside these windows and have a clear view into the room where the high school boys will be naked taking showers.

All of this is completely new to the rest of us. Standing tippy-toe on the ground outside these windows, we are able to see inside where the whole football team is in the process of taking showers. Julie and Ann, Bobby and I are all able to spy on these naked senior high school boys who are old enough to have fully grown penises. This too is an embarrassing episode, but in a different way. Julie and Ann are wide-eyed at what they see, and I hear them murmuring "Wow, look at that" while they are peering in the windows, but I know that my body does not look like these older boys that we are spying on, and I wonder what if anything this might mean to Julie.  We don't ever discuss the event afterwards, but within a year or two, we are no longer going together after Julie meets a big blond guy who is among the Catholic students who have come over to our high school when the Catholic school stops teaching them after 6th grade. I Imagine that Julie, seeing what a big guy she can seduce, pictures him as having the kind of equipment she observed in the senior boys' shower, and perhaps she even finds out for herself that such is the case.

Speaking of male equipment, that summer I go to Boys'

Club summer camp, which includes grades 6-10. This means that many of the boys there are two or three years older than I am. One hot day we are all skinny dipping in the muddy creek where we swim. Jimmy Mansfield is a sophomore guy from my neighborhood who is playing his own made-up game of Jack-in-the-box. He is sitting on the muddy bank with a hard on. He keeps pushing his erect penis down into the mud and watching for a second or two before it snaps up to attention as the upward force of his erection overcomes the viscosity of the mud, all the while laughing madly as his cock keeps snapping up like a catapult and splattering mud around on the other boys. This impresses me considerably because I have never before seen an older boy with a hard-on, and, of course, the force of his erection overcoming the stickiness of the mud is truly impressive, simply from an engineering point of view. Also, I think that his ingenuity in using his cock to fling mud at the others is extremely creative. His game could have been called, not jack-in-the-box, but stick-in-the-mud.

Although there is no television in the small town when and where I am growing up, there is the movie theater uptown, and a ticket only costs 18 cents, so it isn't difficult to scrape up some pennies and go. I have seen most of the movies for kids, starting with Bambi, Dumbo, Snow White and Pinocchio, but now I am loving the Tarzan movies, with Johnny Weismuller as Tarzan. I greatly admire Tarzan's bare-chested male physique and of course I think that Jane is very sexy in her skimpy, ragged dress. I think it is exotic that Tarzan and Jane have a chimp for a pet and almost family member.

Another of my favorites is the klutzy guy trying to do home repairs who constantly falls off the ladder or hits his thumb with the hammer. It isn't Laurel and Hardy but some ordinary guy who is named Mr. Hardway or something like that. This is long before the three stooges, but this guy is very funny.

The movie show is frequently preceded by a news program showing images of the war. The scenes of Japanese planes with close-ups of their pilots look very scary, because the pilots are so slanty-eyed and sinister looking, but this was probably not in the newsreels but in some war movie like Guadalcanal Diary. The newsreels don't show a lot of blood and gore, but there are scenes from the liberation of the Nazi death camps which are horrifying. I see scenes of bulldozers pushing many shrunken naked bodies into trenches. Forever seared into my mind is one picture in these newsreels that shows a trench full of emaciated naked bodies all tangled together. I focus in particular on the face of one dark-haired woman who looks like my mother, and I feel how frail life really is. This image is as vivid in my mind today as in the movie show where I first see it, though at that time I didn't know that this woman in the trench could actually have been Mom had her family stayed in Minsk.

I also enjoy some of the radio programs. My favorite is the

Lone Ranger. When my family is in father's car driving out of Buffalo I persuade them to go out of their way to go past a store where I know there is a full-size model of the Lone Ranger sitting on his white horse, Trigger. Years later when Iam back in graduate school for the second time, I'm reminiscing about this with my architecture school classmate Bob Hoffberger and I tell him about how as a boy I was always so thrilled, not just with the William Tell Overture as the background music, but even more so when, at the end of each program someone asks, after the Lone Ranger has ridden off into the sunset,

"Who **was** that masked man?"

Bob supplies the next statement on the program that I had forgotten. The next speaker always responds by saying,

"Yeah, I wanted to thank him."

My favorite comics are Captain Marvel and Blackhawk. When I read Captain Marvel, I am thrilled when he says: "Shazam" to turn into Captain Marvel, although, strangely, I pronounce the word in my mind with the accent on the first syllable rather than the last, which takes away the whole force of the word when spoken. I identify strongly with Billy Batson because he is a slightly-built boy like me yet has the power to become this powerful superhero just by uttering his magic word. I wish I had a magic word that would make me powerful too.

I like Blackhawk because he has a team of people from all different countries. I remember that there is a black guy, a Swede, an Irishman and I think an Italian. I don't remember if there is a Jewish guy. Since the town where I am growing up is so white bread, I find it exotic to read about all these different people.

But, because my mother doesn't want me to be reading comic books, which she considers "junk", I have to read them in my bedroom, and be prepared to shove them under the mattress if I hear her coming, just like John-boy in the Homecoming.

The comics have ads in them by Charles Atlas, the body-builder, whose real name, unknown to me, is Angelo Siciliano, which exhort me to not be a 97-pound weakling, with an image of a frightened skinny guy on a beach blanket cowering into his girlfriend on the blanket as an arrogant, contemptuous-looking muscular guy runs by and kicks sand onto the blanket and the 97-pound weakling. Even now many years later I can still picture that bully kicking sand in that weakling's face. Since I feel myself to also be a skinny, weak guy, I identify strongly with the ads and start to figure out what I have to do to not be that 97-pound weakling. One powerful answer soon arrives.

It is a warm spring afternoon. I am on my way into the

back door of school after walking the two blocks from lunch at home.  Standing in my way is one of the bullies in my class, Joe Hammerton. He has become a bully to me despite the fact that we had attended each other's birthday parties in the early years of grade school.  He says,

"Where do you think you're going?" as he completely blocks my path.

I'm thinking  Now what do I do?  I'm cornered.  I perceive that Joe is no taller than I am, even though he has a hard body and a square-jawed, tough-looking face. I say:

"Obviously, Joe, I'm going into school after lunch."

He just continues to glare at me defiantly, and as I start to walk past him, he grabs onto me to throw me to the ground, but  I hold on to him also and pull him down with me and we commence to wrestle around on the dusty ground.  Much to my surprise, I feel his body begin to give way as I plant my feet into the dirt behind me and  I am able to actually pin him against the foundation wall with my legs braced against the ground. It turns out that I literally do not know my own strength. This causes a light bulb to turn on in my brain.  I realize that the first step to not being a 97-pound weakling is not to put on weight but rather to overcome the barrier in my own mind.  Hammerton never physically confronts me again.

At age thirteen I have not yet started to masturbate simply

because my testicles have not yet started to produce sperm. My father slyly leaves the Boy Scout Manual open on the workbench to the page where it contains the outrageously false information that masturbation will prevent a boy from maturing, but I pay no attention to that because my friend Peter's father tells him

"95 percent of boys masturbate and the other 5 per cent are liars."

Before I go to sleep at night, my hands caressing my erogenous zones are able to very quickly produce a hard on and it feels most wonderful, like no other feeling I have ever had, but I have not yet been able to produce any jism.

One Monday afternoon in the summertime, I am out at the golf course with Ray Gould and John Peterson looking for golf balls. Ray is in my class but John's a couple of years older. We are all caddies, which is a terrific way to earn money. We can make $7 by carrying one player's bag for 18 holes, and double that if we carry two bags. Monday is Caddie Day, the one day each week when we can actually play on the course because it is officially closed to members and guests. Since none of us has money to spare on golf balls, we find them in the woods around the perimeter of the course. On this particular day, we decide to spend some time looking for golf balls rather than playing, because our supplies of balls are all depleted.

We are always hitting balls into the woods ourselves whenwe play. We have just finished searching in the woods south of the $9^{th-18th}$ fairway and west of the $4^{th-13th}$. Our walk through the woods has paid off handsomely. We have each found over a dozen balls, including several Titleists in like-new condition.

After we have traipsed through the woods, we come out onto the fourth fairway, which slopes down fairly steeply toward the woods on the right which we have just escaped. Ray and John both say simultaneously,

"Let's take a little break", so we all sit down resting on the grass with our feet downhill toward the woods.

John says,

"Well, Grady, as long as we're sitting here, we may as well jack off", and, much to my surprise, both of them take their cocks out of their pants and begin to stroke their impressive hard ons. In a classic case of monkey see -monkey do, I follow their example. I have no problem getting mine hard, and even though I have never experienced ejaculation and have no expectation of doing so now, still my hand keeps going while I hope for my first miracle. After first John, and then Ray, both shoot a rope of their jizz off onto the fairway grass between their legs, I keep up the pretense for a few seconds before giving up. Ray, who is clearly delighted by the realization that I am not yet able to produce jizz, grins at me and mockingly yells,

   "Jaaacker",

stretching out the vowel sound dramatically.  To him, I will be forever known by that name, so he will keep ostentatiously yelling this at me with a big smirk on his face for the entire remaining years of school.  It's a good thing Ray is not taking the college prep courses that I am, so I don't have to suffer with his mockery every day, and probably most of the students who hear him have no idea why he is calling me that.

   As I get into Junior High School, I begin to contract the teen-age curse.  I am very embarrassed by the big pimples I get on my face. None of the acne prescriptions sold in the drugstore do any good.  It sure doesn't do me any good either to pop the pimples and squeeze out the blackheads, but I continue to do so, despite the fact that my face gets splotchy with red marks when I do it. I feel that even with the splotches I still look better without the black heads and pimple heads.  It is depressing, because I can see in the mirror that I am a good-looking guy except for the acne and I would love to have a complexion free of all the disfiguration.  The only saving grace is that so many other students in my school have the same problem, and some of them are quite a bit worse than me.  Still, I feel that I will have to take a 2 or 3-year sabbatical from girls while my acne goes through its normal course.

One experience around my acne is especially excruciating and self-defeating.  My mother is in our living room working on a church project in which she is collaborating with an inner-city congregation and has as a guest a much younger female, who happens to be a beautiful black woman.  I am very attracted to black women because I see them as foreign, exotic, assertive and intensely interesting, so I would love nothing better than to schmooze with her, but, as it happens, the first time I come into our living room and see her planning with my mother, I am going through an especially bad episode of acne and am supremely embarrassed to be with a woman, especially a beautiful, exotic-looking woman like her.  My mom says,

"Meet my friend, Judy",

who gives me a radiant smile as I quickly shake her hand and immediately high-tail it out of the room so that she will not have too long a chance to focus on my complexion, while at the same time agonizing internally that I can't spend some time near her enjoying her beauty and sexiness.  The thing that is so ironic about this is that my mother later leads me to believe that Julie is hurt by my sudden exit, and probably attributes it to her belief that I don't want to see **her** complexion, yet nothing could be further from the truth.

One compensation for my acne is that my testicles are now able to produce sperm, so I am masturbating with great pleasure. I worry that I am doing it too often, so I try to set limits on it. I mark up a calendar with a big X every third day, the X day being the day when it will be OK to jerk off. But it always feels so wonderful that I am very apt to cheat. It will be only the second day and in bed my left hand seems to wander of its own free will onto my erogenous zones, causing my penis to harden rapidly, and then we are off and running at Hialeah. It is odd that I jerk-off left-handed because I am right-handed with everything else except this and dealing cards. I stroke for a few minutes and then stop, foolishly thinking I am going to be able to make it to the next night, but of course my hand soon goes back to it and the supremely beautiful feeling intensifies. After two or three of these stop-and-start-again sequences, I finally can't stand to hold back any longer, and I experience ecstasy as the shot goes way up over my shoulder.

At first I don't need any external stimulation aids, but before long I am doing it while looking at Maidenform bra ads and Petty Girl calendars. This is decades before all the explicit porn becomes as readily available as it is now on the internet. My friend Teddy shares with me a naked picture of his own mother along with some graphic pictures of strangers which he had found in his father's stash of pornographic materials. The picture of his mother is a benign solitary reclining nude pose, almost identical to Manet's famous painting, Olympia, and I can't help but wonder what having possession of it is doing to Teddy's Oedipus complex.

While waiting for my acne to go away, I start to work more aggressively on my resolve not to be a ninety seven pound weakling. I have been going to the local boys club, where I have learned pool, and I go there to play it after school, thereby ignoring the warnings of the Music Man. While playing pool with Teddy one afternoon, he tells me,

" Grady, do you realize that this club has a weight room where we can lift weights and build-up our bodies?"

I am still too reluctant to be around other stronger boys even with my friend Teddy there, so I limit myself to simply observing the lifting equipment the boys club has , then start saving up to buy my own second-hand set of weights. I don't investigate Angelo Siciliano's theory of dynamic tension but simply decide to go on a campaign of lifting weights at home to build up my muscles. I feel that lifting weights is a private activity like jerking off, despite, or maybe because of, my experience on the golf course with Ray and John.

In order to lift weights I have to be a bit of a masochist, because the strain of lifting weights is actually kind of painful. The strain of pushing my muscles to do more and more lifts is similar to pain, but I soon realize that it is a positive type of pain that goes away as soon as I complete the series of lifts. Using the curls to develop my biceps is my favorite exercise and the one that I think is most important, because my arm muscles are most prominent when wearing short sleeve shirts in the warm seasons.

At the same time as I am working to build up my body, I am reading the Bible from cover to cover, after being challenged by my mother to read it when I express to her my developing atheism.  My sisters and I have been attending Sunday School, but the only parts of it I like are Palm Sunday and the 23rd psalm.  Palm Sunday is cool because we all get to bring home these fun long dry reeds. But parts of Sunday school are repelling, especially Mr. Samson, who shows us crude, almost cartoon depictions of Jesus and his disciples all standing around in robes in the desert.  The revolting thing about Mr. Samson is that, while he is trying to teach us about Jesus, I can't take my eyes off the strands of mucous constantly occupying the corners of his mouth, just like the way you can't keep your fingers from probing around a sore on your body.

When I ask my mother:

" What do these people standing around in robes in the desert so long ago have to do with my life?",

she doesn't try to persuade me of anything but simply suggests:

" Why don't you read the Bible and then make up your own mind?"

So I proceed to read four or five pages every night, until, after more than a year, I have completed the whole thing, while absorbing very little of it. Reading it is an exercise just like lifting weights, something to be endured in order to get a rewarding benefit, although the weights have a much more positive effect than reading the bible. This is years before I read Thomas Paine's "Common Sense", in which he completely rejects the bible as ancient myth, and moreover, myth that shows the almighty to be cruel and sadistic. Yet, Paine still believes in a beneficent God. It is also years before I read Bishop Spong, who shows how the New Testament, written by Jewish intellectuals, actually follows the calendar of Jewish tradition. It is also years before I hear the lecture by Julian Huxley in college which cements my beliefs as a full-blown atheist.

I am able to tone up my muscles by cross country running and playing golf. This results in smooth, nice-looking muscles which are just naturally part of my body, not the exaggerated bulging ones that "Semi" had at Philmont Scout Ranch a few years earlier. Our group of boy scouts from my town and surrounding towns had been paired up with a group from Jersey, and Semi was among them. He had built up a weight-lifter's body, showing nothing but muscles. Using the same tactic I had used by palling up with John Kane years earlier, I glombed onto Semi on that trip for the same reason.  He was called Semi because he reminded other guys of a semi-trailer truck.

While serving as a great body guard for me, he is anything but a role model.  I have no desire to have the gross, bulging muscles that he has, and, in fact, they prove to be of little practical use when our group plays a game of pickup football with a group from Texas that we run into at one of the campsites at Philmont.  Their leader, a muscular, tough-looking and tough-talking fireplug of a guy, who brags about how he and his buddies are constantly showing their local "niggers" where they stand, ends up pushing Semi all over the field.  Semi's artificially built-up muscles are totally ineffective when put up against a tough rancher from Texas.

This proves to me that weight-lifting is only one component of building up an attractive, muscular body, and should never be used to such an extreme as to build up an artificially exaggerated set of muscles like Semi, or like the beach bully in the Charles Atlas ads.

That Philmont trip, by the way, results in a great romantic disappointment.  On the Santa Fe going across Kansas, I am blown away by the extremely flat country where you can see all the way to the horizon in any direction, like the scene in North by Northwest when Cary Grant gets off the bus in Minnesota.  But also I meet a cute little farm girl named Jody, who has the most interesting mid-western drawl. I have never talked with a girl who sounds like her. We flirt and schmooze for a day or so on the train until she has to get off in Abilene. Before she gets off, we exchange addresses, so I can correspond with her while I am in New Mexico. In our few letters, we agree to meet at the railroad terminal in Kansas City on my way back east.

When our train arrives back at Kansas City, I get one of the shocks of my life when I see Jody there, but she is all wrapped up in very excited, animated conversation with Neil Mulder, one of the nondescript Jersey guys, who had not impressed me in any way while we were at Philmont. He dresses in dull ill-fitting, mis-matched clothes, is not handsome, and even exhibits a bit of b.o. She pays no attention to me whatsoever, and in fact does not even acknowledge my presence when I approach them. I find out from him later that he had also met Jody on the train and had corresponded with her as I had, and had arranged to meet her at the train station on his way back east, just as I had.

Cute little innocent farm girl Jody turns out to be a two-timing Jezebel. That teaches me a valuable lesson about women, except that I have no idea what the lesson really is, other than to use a little caution. Fortunately It is not that painful a lesson because she proves herself to be stupid enough to two-time me with such a total dwebe.

My acne is finally fading away and I'm getting to be a honcho. I get very good grades, but I'm not a teacher's pet. I take pride in getting top grades while at the same time getting low "honor points," which have nothing to do with honor but simply with being on good behavior in class in the opinion of the teacher. This gives me street cred with the regular guys in the class. While I don't play football or basketball, which are the main sports that get attention and status, still I am on the Cross Country and Golf teams and I play trumpet in the school band, which leads to my forming a dance band to play at school dances. We call ourselves the "Stardusters", and have matching black cardboard music stands to use at dances with that logo in white letters. I am also elected Vice-President of our senior class, second to Smiley Youngman who is by far the most popular kid in the school. No wonder he is always smiling. Still, in our class yearbook I am voted as "most versatile", which translates to 'jack of all trades, master of none', like my father's favorite opera character, the baritone factotum in The Barber of Seville.

The most important event in high school for me is that I start going steady with Sheila Wilson during the last semester of senior year. During our junior year, we had both been members of the Service Club headquartered in the Presbyterian Church. On Sunday nights, they have a weekly social involving meetings about club programs and activities, and a supper typically consisting of tuna fish or egg salad sandwiches on white bread with the crusts cut off, along with soda and green salad.  Years later I love to eat those same kind of sandwiches when donating blood for the Red Cross, and, in fact, it is mainly the lure of those sandwiches that induces me to go to the blood drive in the first place.   The artist friend I acquire in later years in the "New Group" might playfully refer to these as "sanqwidges", thereby making fun of the pronunciation by some of the uneducated people she worked with.

Every once in a while, the service club also has a dance, using record collections lent by some of the members.  Sheila is not supermodel material, but she is intelligent and attractive, with a nice full figure, and I greatly enjoy having conversations with her.  We seem to have a similar sense of humor, sharing laughs about some of the foolish attitudes and behavior of our teachers and classmates.

At one of these dances on a cold, January night,  I get up my courage enough to ask Sheila,

"Would you like to dance?"   She says,

"Sure, Grady", so we get out onto the dance floor.  What totally amazes me about Sheila is that she is as light as a feather in my arms.  She seems to 'float like a butterfly' without 'stinging like a bee' as she follows my dance moves smoothly and effortlessly, to the point that I don't have to use any pressure with my arms to speak of.  I had gone to our local dancing school with many of the other kids, and I'm a pretty good dancer if I do say so myself.  As I dance with my right hand resting comfortably in the small of Sheila's back, she is magically floating weightlessly right with me all the way.  This is a revelation.  I had experienced dancing with some girls who were practically inert, with my having to make a real effort to pull them around the dance floor, like trying to drag a heavy tank.

It takes me until weeks later, in the springtime, before I get the nerve to call her up and ask her out on an actual date. My mom encourages me by saying,

"Faint heart ne'er won fair lady",

and, since I no more want  to have a faint heart than to be a 97 pound weakling,  I dial  Sheila's family's number.  When Sheila's mother answers,   I say:

"This is Grady Markell. Can Sheila come to the phone?"

I am relieved when her mother says,

" Of course, I'll get her."

Sheila says "Hello".

"Hi, Sheila, it's Grady Markell."

Her "Hi, Grady", given in a bright positive voice, encourages me further.

I say, "I was wondering if you would be interested in going to the movies with me Friday night?"

Sheila asks me, "what's playing?"

I say "I think it's An American in Paris, with Leslie Caron."

She says, "sure, I'd love to see it".

Friday night we are sitting in a pretty crowded movie theater. At one particularly emotional sequence in the movie, our hands seemingly come together as though they had their own volition, and her hand is so soft, warm and giving off some kind of energy that I suddenly feel that I am connected to some mysterious, powerful force. As Sheila's hand gently squeezes mine with such warmth, I instantly know that I want to get much more involved with her. This is like that scene later in "Sleepless in Seattle", where Tom Hanks' wife, before they knew each other, takes his hand while he is helping her out of a car, and he instantly knows just from the touch of her hand that she is the woman for him.

Seeing that movie years later is when I am reminded of holding Sheila's hand years before, because Tom Hanks taking her hand while helping her out of the car is the major generating plot device at the beginning of that film. Hanks is also an architect, just about the only time in any dramatic production where I have seen that the protagonist is incidentally an architect, other than Howard Roark in the Fountainhead and Wilbur, the owner of Mr. Ed, the famous talking horse ('a horse is a horse, of course, of course'),  and of course in the Fountainhead the architecture is anything but incidental.

After the movie, we drive out in my family's car to Emerson Park, where we park in a secluded area, and, without any delay or standing-on-ceremony, begin to make out like tall dogs.  There is no actual sex, of course, because we didn't do that in high school in those days.  But her kisses are long and intense, deep and deeply felt, and our tongues mingle, plus there is a little surreptitious feeling-up going on, so that we are totally excited with each other and totally turned on. With the benefit of a little hindsight, I realize that I should have asked her right away to go steady, but I don't think of that until after I drop her off in the driveway of her house. Then I figure I can cover that step on our next date, which we had already made for the following Friday night at my house

Sheila never tells me that she had also been dating our mutual friend and classmate, Tim Swan.  The most famous thing about Tim is his old blue 1937 Studebaker which he calls the "blue beetle."  Sheila and I are among Tim's friends who ride around in the blue beetle from time to time, stopping every so often to buy 50 cents or a dollar's worth of gas.

On the following Friday,  as soon as we have settled down into the couch in front of the fireplace in my family's living room,  I cuddle in close and ask  Sheila,

" How about you and I go steady?"

She could have hit me in the forehead with a two-by-four when she says,

"Sorry, Grady, but I just agreed two days ago to go steady with Tim Swan."

I am completely flabbergasted by this news and I chokingly respond,

"But you never told me you were even dating him".

She apologizes, and says,

"I just want to have a steady dating relationship with someone I like, and when you didn't ask me to go steady but Tim did, I agreed. If you had asked me first, I would have agreed to go steady with you instead.  I didn't want to tell you this over the telephone so I came ahead to meet you tonight so I could tell you in person."

Here on the very same meeting when I hope to start going steady with Sheila, she tells me that she cannot date me at all. This puts a very large wet blanket over my feelings for Sheila. Things have apparently moved too fast for my deliberate style, although until that moment I haven't realized that I am especially cautious. In fact, I always thought that I was pretty decisive.

Sheila turns out to be even more practical, opportunistic and decisive than I am, and I'm thinking maybe Sheila is as much of a two-timing Jezebel as western Jody was. It's only later that I realize the obvious fact that actually I have no claim on her after only one date, and she is being extremely forthright and honest.

During the fall season, I begin dating 'bloodless' Donna Calvin, so nicknamed because her skin and hair are so pale that she is like an albino. Her almost white curly light blond hair with the pale skin creates a very unique and rather spectacular effect. I meet her as a result of her supposedly being the girlfriend of a buddy of one of the musicians from Buffalo that play in my dance band.

When we were first starting to play the sheet music with popular tunes of the day, we had a skeleton crew of me and Smiley on trumpet and Tim Swan on clarinet and alto sax, along with Dan Naughton on piano and Gene Fishman on drums. None of us played with any real jazz feeling and we didn't even have a bass player. This compares with full seventeen-piece dance bands like Stan Kenton's that have four trumpets, five saxes, four trombones and a rhythm section of drums, bass, guitar and piano.

One afternoon, after some pretty terrible attempts to produce a dance-band sound, Tim says to me;

"At my last saxophone lesson in Buffalo, my teacher told me that he has a couple of other students from  Buffalo that might be interested in joining our band, an alto sax player and a tenor saxophonist." I say,

"Wow, Tim, that would be terrific!  A more complete harmonic sax section would be the most important way to get a fuller dance band sound.  Why don't you arrange for them to come out some afternoon and try out with us, even though in reality we'll be trying out with them".

A week later, these two guys show up at our afternoon practice.  The alto sax player is named Ben Burwell, with a short, stocky figure and black, curly hair. He looks like a serious scientist or college professor.   The tenor sax player looks like a football player and has dirty blonde straight hair. I ask him what his name is and he says,

"By great co-incidence, my name is Mel Torme, just like the jazz singer".

Being as naïve as I am, and also not wanting to incur the risk of annoying him by questioning his name while our band is really trying out with these two more experienced sax players, I take it at face value.  The first chart we try to play is Glen Miller's "In the mood," and when we reach the tenor sax solo, Mel literally blows me away by honking the ride out just the way it sounds on the record. From that point on, Ben and Mel are members of our band, the Stardusters become a viable band to play at school dances, and I'm proud that we have such a great tenor sax player as Mel Torme.

Several years later, I'm traveling around Buffalo with an arrogant kid named Mike who got the job because he is the son of one of the company executives. I am on a summer job working for the gas company after my second year of college. We deliver gas appliances to apartments in Buffalo. During our trips to the delivery jobs, we are constantly arguing about religion, Mike being a Catholic. He says, channelling Thomas Acquinas ,

"The way you know there is a god is, if you are walking in the desert and see a watch, you know that some intelligent mind must have made this watch."

"So what?"

"Well, that's like seeing the world and knowing that some intelligent mind must have created it".

"But then, who created God?"

"God has always existed."

" So, maybe the world has always existed". And so on and so on, ad infinitum.

One afternoon we are told to deliver some generator parts to a plant in Cheektowaga, which is a smelly industrial area of the city. We are driving by a lot of three-story residential buildings with a store on the ground floor, packed tightly together with at most a driveway in between, and sheathed in fake yellow brick siding which is actually just cheap, peeling yellow-brown particle board with a brick pattern etched into the surface. We are smelling the very pervasive, piercing nauseating odor from the industries around there and I wonder how anyone can shop and work in such an environment, never mind actually living there.

We come to a small industrial building belonging to the gas company. Mike and I go inside looking for the guy to whom we are supposed to make the delivery, wandering through a series of dark room

Finally we come to one especially dark room where a number of men in dull grey work clothes are working at one long bench assembling generators. It's like we have suddenly stumbled into a prison or a German concentration camp where the inmates are performing demeaning chores in very dim light. Suddenly, one of them calls out " Grady, what are you doing here?", and I dimly recognize Mel Torme at one of the work stations along the single bench.

We had not seen each other for over two years, so there wasn't much we could share, just the usual meaningless small talk that all of us indulge in on such occasions. After a few minutes, Mike says,

"Grady, we've got to get going",

so I give Mel a quick hug and then Mike and I are on the way to our next delivery. During my brief conversation with Mel, I experience a shock when I see Mel's ID plate on the shelf in front of his work station, and read the name "Mel Zumbroski".

It is only then that I come to the full realization of something I had only dimly thought about. Mel is actually a working stiff from the Polish section of Buffalo who just happens to be a great saxophone player. -

This background never registered while he was in the WASP suburbs playing in a band with college-bound kids who were the sons of businessmen and professionals. Wedded to this realization in my mind is the chagrin at knowing what an idiot I have been for having accepted for several years, hook, line and sinker, the outlandish story that this guy's name was the same as the famous jazz singer, Mel Torme.

One afternoon, Ben and Mel are accompanied by this spectacular pale blond girl who is introduced as Donna Calvin, being the girlfriend of one of Mel's friends, which is my first introduction to bloodless Donna. Her skin is so pale and translucent that it provides me with my nickname for her. If I were among Jewish companions, she would be idolized as the ultimate Shiksa.

After hanging around at some of our practice sessions and flirting with me there, she seems to be willing to go out with me even though she is still supposedly the girlfriend of this other guy in the city. I never do figure this situation out, and I'm not sure whether I might be putting myself in danger by going out with a tough city guy's girlfriend.

On about my fourth or fifth date with bloodless Donna, we are attending a New Year's Eve "progressive" dinner party, where they have an appetizer course at one house, then proceed to the next house for the soup course, on to a third residence for the entrée, and then to yet another house for dessert. It turns out that Sheila is at the party also, but not with Tim. She is with a junior guy we all know named Dick Holmes, known to the girls as "Hands Holmes" because of the propensity of his hands to be wandering around on their bodies where they are not welcome. I can't figure out what Sheila is doing at the party with this guy. Surely she is not interested in being constantly felt up against her will, but then again, maybe it wouldn't be against her will.

After the dessert course at Dan Naughton's house, his parents have disappeared and the kids are paired off around the house with the opportunity to do some serious necking with their dates. I am lying on a couch with bloodless Donna's tongue in my ear. She is the first girl I have ever known who uses that particular tactic to turn guys on. It must be something that Buffalo kids do. It provides a tickling sensation that also causes me to get a hard-on.

After necking for awhile, the party starts to break up, and somehow I suddenly find myself alone in the entry vestibule with Sheila. Sheila brightly says to me,

"Hi, Grade, are you having fun?"

I'm sure she says this because she had seen me on the couch doing some serious necking with bloodless Donna.

"Why are you here with hands Holmes instead of Tim?"

Sheila says,

"Tim would rather hang out with his buddies working on the Blue Beetle than go out with me on New Years' Eve. I'll bedamned if I'm going to be left home alone on New Years' Eve, so I put pressure on Dick to take me to this party. Believe me, I have no intention of making out with hands Holmes or even going out with him again, but I am no longer going steady with Tim."

After she delivers this news, Sheila and I are both standing there foolishly grinning at each other when, before you can say "Jack Robinson", we simultaneously move toward each other and start kissing, and we keep on kissing for several minutes.  At this point, Dan Naughton, whose house we are kissing in, who plays piano in my dance band, and who will become class Valedictorian, happens by on the way to seeing guests out the door, and discovers us in the vestibule in full embrace, but of course not in flagrante delicto.  After presumably having seen me on the couch with bloodless Donna only a little earlier, Dan says to both of us with pointed sarcasm,

"some people will kiss **anyone**".

He could have no way of knowing that Sheila and I would, within a few years, be ensconced in a lasting marriage.

From that point on, I save my skin from a potential beating by leaving ear-licking bloodless Donna to her tough city boyfriend, and Sheila and I begin steadily dating, constantly in each other's company all during the second semester of senior year.  We are also in several classes together.  In Miss Boyer's algebra class, she sits right behind me.  Sometime much later she confesses to me that, when we took written tests in that class, she would always surreptitiously peer over my shoulder to check the answers on my paper before turning in her own paper, which she had already completed.  She tells me,

"I just wanted to be sure that my answers were correct, because I knew that yours would be.  I never had to change any of my own answers."

I am surprised by this because I know that Sheila is very smart and a very good student. She is just showing how practical and careful she is, and forever after I observe Sheila's habit of checking and double-checking everything. In fact, she finishes high school as the top girl academically, fourth overall, while I finish as the class Salutatorian, even though I am never officially recognized as such.

The reason for this non-recognition is that the school principal, Tom Morgan, is very good friends with the parents of Ned Mayberry, one of the smart kids in our class. Based on incomplete grade scores in April of our senior year, Mr. Morgan prematurely announces to a class assembly

"Dan Naughton will be class Valedictorian and Ned Mayberry will be the Salutatorian."

As I hear this, I have no idea where I rank in grade standings. I know that I have had good academic marks throughout school, although not so with behavior points in Junior High School, but I have no idea where I stand relative to other students, so I have no reason to believe that there is anything wrong with the principal's announcement.

As it turns out, at the time of Mr. Morgan's announcement I am next in order behind Ned Mayberry, and I finish strong on my final exams and just beat out Ned for second place. At graduation, Mr. Morgan, having painted himself into a corner by his premature April announcement of his friend's son's standing, which has now turned out not to be true, and evidently not being man enough to acknowledge his April mistake, finesses the situation by not announcing a Salutatorian at all. He simply states that the class has three top boys, that Dan, Ned and I have finished as the top three, and that Dan is Valedictorian. He doesn't even admit that I have finished ahead of Ned. My mother is furious at this gross display of favoritism to the disadvantage of her son, but lets sleeping dogs lie and doesn't make a stink about it.

I am in my second year at State College. Sheila has gone off to her own university in upstate New York. We only see each other on vacations and on occasional visits to each other's school. We understand that we will date others to gain experience but expect that we will probably end up together after college. I have pledged to a fraternity that combines socially adept students with good athletes- not the most prestigious fraternity on campus, but still a good one. I believe that It is a good idea to be in a fraternity because of the social connections and the great venue for parties that it provides. Not the least of the considerations for this decision was the opportunity to play bridge, euchre or chess at lunchtime and sometimes in the afternoon.

I am at the fraternity one afternoon close to the end of sophomore year, with the guys smoking some joints, when Joe Macleod's female friend- not a girlfriend- shows up. She is a senior while the rest of us are sophomores. She and Joe are from the same town and were friends in high school. Samantha acts right at home in the fraternity with no other women around, and even her nickname "Sam" is of course also a common boy's name. Her flamboyant personality and attitude of easy familiarity at the fraternity begins to annoy me, so I commence to make sarcastic comments. I say to her,

"Are you really a woman, or just one of the boys?"

She angrily responds to me,

"What do you know about it, Grady, have you never met an assertive female"?

We go on in this manner, with Sam apparently being intrigued and challenged, and even apparently turned on, by my expressions of sarcasm and hostility. After another joint, she comes over and sits on my lap in mock, playful annoyance, and then, somehow, we begin to kiss. This surprises both of us as we continue with the kissing, and I even put my hand on her ample tits. Sam says:

"Man o man could I do a dance on you! I say,

"Let's try out that theory"

as we are on the way to my room at the fraternity. While we are getting undressed, Sam says,

" You look better and better the more clothes you take off".

In order to find out what Sam means by doing a dance on me, I forego the missionary position and let Sam get on top of me. Her choreography turns out to be a little too frenetic for me, which seems consistent with her general personality. Not only does she appear to be trying to strangle my cock, but she seems intent on grinding it right off my body. I manage to slow her down enough to reach a climax, and our little soiree is quickly over. In fact, it is over so fast that I may as well have said," Wham, bam, thank you ma'am." Despite her admiring words about my naked body, the encounter has not been very pleasant, and I am able to steer clear of Sam for the remainder of the semester.  She is more of a meat grinder than a woman.

Until much, much later, I never do tell Sheila about my lightning-fast roll in the hay with Sam, because I know that Sheila is maintaining her status as a virgin until her wedding, in the traditional, old-fashioned way.  She is not necessarily expecting me to do the same, but, if we do end up getting married, I know that she will be much happier to believe that she is first for me just as I am first for her.  Since that fast fuck with Sam carries with it no emotional component, and I never see her again afterwards, it seems pretty insignificant to me and not worth roiling Sheila up for nothing.

During summer vacation after the end of that year, I am naturally looking to earn as much money as I can to help with expenses in my upcoming Junior year of college.  Sheila has a full time job as a clerk in the Department Store in Buffalo.  She gets the job because the father of one of her closest high school friends is the manager of the whole store.  With Sheila working full time,  naturally I feel more pressure to secure a good job of my own.   Based on my second place finish in high school, I have received scholarships to pay tuition, but that doesn't take care of  food, clothes, transportation and entertainment at college.  I could get a laborer's job with my Dad's  construction company, but I know that his business is way down due to the big real estate collapse the previous year, which has depressed the whole construction industry, even public projects like schools. This means that I am not really needed and I don't like the idea of getting paid to do unnecessary make-work.

So my friend Jeff and I take a job for our political science professor, doing inside finishing work at Professor Hansen's home. Professor Hansen and his wife, Gloria, are a good twenty five years older than Jeff and me. Gloria does not work outside the home, so she is in the house while we are working. The first morning on the job I am doing some painting on the kitchen cabinets while Jeff is working in one of the bedrooms. Because it's a very hot, muggy day, and the home is not air-conditioned, I take off my shirt to be reasonably comfortable. Professor Hanson's wife comes into the kitchen to watch me working, and she immediately engages me in meaningless conversation. Gloria is an attractive redhead. She says,

"I understand that you kids are in my husband's political science class."

"Yeah, that class is one of our favorites."

"What's your name?"

"It's Grady Markell."

Within a few minutes after I have removed my shirt, and I

am carrying on this meaningless conversation with Mrs. Hanson, I realize that she has gotten up very close to me watching my painting work on the kitchen cabinet. Suddenly I feel her breasts pressing against my right arm. Assuming this is an unintended mistake, I say "sorry" and shift away from her to the left. But then, a few minutes later, I again feel her tits pressing against my arm, and, embarrassed, I hurriedly excuse myself to use the bathroom. By the time I return, Gloria Hanson and her tits have gone, so I can resume my painting work. I never see her again during that job, and never mention this incident with Gloria Hanson to anyone except Sheila, who thinks it is very funny. Sheila laughs when I say,

"Apparently Gloria is not getting what she wants and needs from the Professor."

This isn't my best summer job. The best one is the summer I work for the steel company in Buffalo owned by Sheila's best friend's father. The factory floor has a number of different machines, including one where the worker sits up top over a very large revolving boiler. His job is to weld the seams on the boiler. Other workers perform other jobs with the machines that are part of the boiler-making process at various stations around the factory floor. My job is to collect the trash produced by each workman. This means that I am always on the move around the plant rather than being confined to one place. I enjoy schmoozing with the men on my daily rounds, especially one guy who is a movie buff. The only thing is, he doesn't pay any attention to the substance of the movie plots or even to the acting. His sole focus is to notice where something in a scene is out of place and doesn't belong there. He's delighted in being able to spot flaws in the sets.

Sometimes I arrive home from Buffalo still in dirty work clothes from my job, but I need to go to the Fisher "brothers" to get a haircut. I put that in quotes because I have since wondered whether they were really brothers. One of them is a square-faced hard-looking guy while Duane is a good looking guy with softer features and with a very gentle voice and hands. They don't look anything like brothers. In these days gays are definitely in the closet.

I like both of them, but I prefer Duane because he has such a soft touch. One evening when I am there in dirty work clothes after coming back from my summer job, I apologize to Duane about it, but he says, "Yes, but it's **clean** dirt." That comment brings tears to my eyes because he turns something I am apologizing for into something I should be proud of.

One thing I especially like about being at the Fisher brothers is that they have magazines I never get to see at home or school, including Esquire, which includes the Petty Girl illustrations, where the girls always sport large pointy tits. This is a great contrast to Titter magazine which I see while in college, where they show nothing but huge bulging breasts in low necklines ad nauseum, except that I believe that is also the magazine which features one of my favorite cartoon series, sometimes on the cover, the one showing a guy walking or driving on the street watching a girl walking by with huge pointy tits in a tight dress with a very low slung dress  and the guy's eyes are bulging impossibly far out of his head and his tongue is hanging out of his mouth like a large slobbering dog.

My really favorite thing at the Fisher brothers is the painting on the wall showing a group of all different kinds of dog breeds playing poker, with the bulldog in the foreground passing a card to the dog on his left by means of his foot, with the card wedged between his toes and a cigar clamped in his teeth.

# CHAPTER TWO


# A BEGINNING

I have graduated from college with a Bachelor of Arts degree, I am newly married to Sheila and I am working in my father's construction business. I have been lucky to stay out of the army. I had gotten a student deferment while in college, and then, as soon as Sheila and I are married, I get her pregnant, which entitles me to a deferment as a father. The most memorable thing from college for me are the good news and bad news inscriptions in stone on both sides of the entrance to the college library.

On the left is the good news. The inscription reads:

"Here is the history of man's hunger for truth, goodness and beauty leading him slowly on through flesh to spirit, from bondage to freedom, from war to peace."

On the right is the bad news. The inscription reads:

"Here is the history of human ignorance, error, superstition and waste recorded by human intelligence for the admonition of wiser ages still to come."

The construction company builds schools and community colleges and many smaller commercial projects. I am project manager of two or three projects at a time. Sheila has a college degree in Sociology, so her job in the Social Security Administration provides a welcome supplement to my earnings from the construction company, until she gets into the sixth month of her pregnancy.

It is in the evening a couple of months later.  My face is slowly approaching Laurel Sayles' naked body in the motel room and she says to me in surprise:

"Grady, are you going to love me **that** way?

Laurel is the cute little southern girl who is our new receptionist in the construction company.  Her full given name is probably "Laureline", and she is one of the most seductive women I have ever met.  She has that typical southern politeness, saying "Yes, sir, and no, sir" to the men she speaks with in her sweet southern accent, giving the unmistakable impression that their every wish is her command.  After only a couple of weeks on the job, she has seduced me into a motel room with her for one purpose only.

She is a dancer in her older sister's ballet company and has beautiful legs like Cyd Charisse, but when she takes her clothes off, I am practically struck dumb by the fact that, except for her nipples,  she has the chest of a young boy.  Her nipples are those of a woman, full size as I expected, but they are like gumdrops sitting on a flat plate.  Perhaps because I have no interest in being in bed with a boy, I am not able to fuck her, so she expresses by her question her disappointment that she is not about  to receive the full penetration which she craves.

Despite her indication of being let down before I even

commence the appetizer,  I proceed to greatly enjoy a three-course meal in the entire erogenous zone between her legs, causing her to have one orgasm after another as she squeezes my head with her beautiful, strong legs.  It's as though my head is in a vise, but a very enjoyable, soft one.  Each time her legs squeeze my neck, I feel a great rush of satisfaction and pleasure to be enveloped by such gorgeous gams and to be the cause of such intense pleasure on her part.  Of course, this turns out to be a once-in-a-lifetime experience, because what Laurel seems to have an insatiable craving for is the male member fully developed for business, and she doesn't have much concern with who is the owner of that member. Laurel is soon graciously seducing an endless series of men with her enticing southern manners, while working for a different employer.

I never tell Sheila about my evening with Laurel until many years later, lying that I had to work late that evening, using the same old tired excuse cheating spouses have used for eons.

My parents have retired to Berkeley, California. Now in order to see them, Sheila and I have to make a cross-country flight. As the son of the owner, I have worked my way up rapidly to be head of the construction company, which requires that I spend most of my time in the office behind a desk. I have a four-man staff consisting of an assistant, two project managers and an estimator, plus a bookkeeper and a secretary to help me run the company, but I quickly begin to chafe at being inside so much of the time, rather than out in the field on a job, which is where I really like to be.

In May, Sheila and I and our two sons take off a few days and fly out to the coast to visit my folks. We depart New York from the new TWA terminal at JFK, which has just been completed by the architect Eero Saarinen the previous year. When I walk into the building, I am completely blown away by the majestic, sweeping architecture. All of the curving forms are suggestive, inside and out, of a large bird about to take flight.

I have seen plenty of pretty good architecture in Buffalo, New York City and Connecticut, both in connection with my construction work and just in general, but nothing to compare with this building by Eero Saarinen. I am so inspired by the fantastic architecture that I begin to germinate ideas of a new career. I am only 30 years old, certainly young enough to start out in a new direction. In my innermost thoughts during this trip, I think about little else. While enjoying the gorgeous scenery of the bay area, I still look forward to the trip back to that building, when I will get the opportunity to marvel once more at the fabulous structure.

Eero Saarinan's TWA Terminal, JFK Airport, New York

Yet, of course, no one who visits the bay area of San Francisco spends much time there thinking about being anywhere else.  The scenery is so gorgeous and there is so much to enjoy and experience while there.  The character of the wide ethnic variety of people is so cosmopolitan yet friendly, open and tolerant, that one cannot help but feel welcomed while in the bay area.  On the flight out, Sheila and I read copies of the S.F. Gate and other bay area publications which had been sent to me by my father so as to acclimate Sheila and me to the special ambiance of the bay area.  We are both totally amazed at the variety of groups and causes that appear in the papers.  It looks like any person, no matter how weird, and no matter what their politics or religion,  can find a group or organization in which to share any interest or predilection that they might have, including something as peculiar as foot fetishism.

When we get to California,  I notice  the tremendous difference from Connecticut in the way land is valued.  In Connecticut, I am used to the zoning laws which typically require for residential property something as much as a fifty ft. setback for the house from the front and rear property lines and between ten and twenty five ft. from the side property lines.  While we are driving  up to the Berkeley hills in our rental car, I say to Sheila,

"Isn't it amazing that we are seeing upscale homes with a great view that are practically right next to each other, with almost no side yards?  These are million dollar homes on postage-stamp sized lots."

Sheila realizes what I am saying, but her response is peremptory about my point.  She says,

"Yes, and look at all the beautiful flowers and shrubbery.  I wish we had so many varieties of flowering plants in Connecticut!"

My parents' house is very strange by Connecticut standards.  It has a single-car garage on the lower level right in the front of the house, but the garage floor is about 15 feet higher than the street and the concrete driveway is extremely steep, certainly far steeper than the maximum 15 per cent grade allowed in Connecticut.  I ask my dad,

" How can you possibly drive your car up this driveway?"

"Well, I won't even find out about that until I can find a place for all this junk that is filling the garage right now."

It is true, the garage is crammed with half-built furniture, indoor and outdoor tools and equipment, boxes full of extra clothes, dishes and home furnishings and god knows what else.  I say,

"Pop, It will be a cold day in hell before you ever get this garage cleaned out enough to fit a car into it."  He doesn't argue with me.

The main level of the house is up a full set of stairs from the garage floor level, one outside and one inside, but when you reach the top, you are well-rewarded.  As we walk into the living room,  featuring large windows across the entire width of the house, which look out to the west over San Francisco Bay,  Sheila exclaims in excitement,

"Grade, Look, there is the Golden Gate Bridge in the distance!"

I also marvel at this amazing view.  The house looks over the top of the houses across the street to a view of the entire northern end of San Francisco Bay, with the sparkling lights of El Cerrito on the near side of the water, Alcatraz far out into the water, Angel Island to the right, and, indeed, there is the magnificent and monumental Golden Gate Bridge in distant full view on the far side of the bay!

While in Berkeley, Sheila and I enjoy many rubbers of bridge with my parents, while enjoying the view of the bay from their window. I don't mention to Mom or Dad my thinking about trying to become an architect, in part because I haven't even mentioned it yet to Sheila. It's just been germinating in my own mind. I figure it will be best not to tell my folks about it until as, if and when it becomes a reality.

As we are sitting in the return plane on the airport tarmac, the plane's sound system is playing Bach's third Brandenberg concerto with excellent fidelity. I am thinking how classy this airline is to be playing such a beautiful classical piece of music, and it opens my ears to the wonders of Bach. I had never before heard such fantastic and satisfying chord progressions, except for the alto sax solo played by Paul Desmond on 'Lonesome Road' with Dave Brubeck's quartet, and he probably got that from Bach anyway. Hearing the Brandenburg concerto broadens my music appreciation beyond Mozart, Beethoven, Brahms, St. Saens and Dvorak. I had been a late comer to classical music. When at one point I share with my sister Elaine my love of Tchaikovsky's Romeo and Juliet Overture, she says sarcastically,

"Yeah, I used to like that when I was a sophomore in high school".

On the trip, from my window seat, I marvel at the abrupt transition from the Rockies to the great plains, and, after travelling much further east, I understand why the plains are called 'great'. It is a clear day, and I can clearly discern the 100 mile quadrants that had been mapped out on the land when the northwest territory was settled.

Arriving back at JFK, I am once again blown away by Saarinen's TWA building, and I decide then and there that I am going to apply to an architecture school and try to become an architect. I realize that, in order to afford the tuition and other expenses of school, I will have to keep the construction company going to generate income, and in order to do that, I must be able to go there every day and keep things running smoothly, even if I do have to delegate most of the responsibility to my subordinates.

I finally share what I have been thinking with Sheila on the way driving back to Connecticut. I say to her out of the clear blue,

"Guess what, Sheila, I want to go back to school to become an architect."

Sheila knows me well enough to know I am dead serious, so she says,

"Grade, even though that shocks me to a degree, I am not completely surprised. On this trip you have made me acutely aware of how you reacted to the terminal building in New York, and I certainly know how ambitious you are. You realize, though, that this would mean three or more years of school, even assuming that you can get admitted, and that we would both have to keep working while you are in school."

" Sure, Sheila, I understand that, but I believe we can do it if you are willing."

Sheila says,

"Do you also realize that this could mean going to an architecture school outside of Connecticut. I don't like the sound of that! I don't want our kids to have to start up again in another school. They've had enough trouble as it is making friends where we are. God forbid we would have to subject them to a new start all over again in a different town."

"Sheila, I completely agree with you. I won't even apply to Risdy or to any of the schools in Massachusetts or New York."

Sheila asks, " But, Grade, what architecture schools are there in Connecticut? Are there any other than Yale? I can't believe that you could get into Yale."

" I don't know if I can either, but I'll soon find out."

I do soon find out that Yale is indeed the only architecture school in Connecticut at this time, so that's where I apply. I have no idea whether I stand a ghost of a chance at being admitted, but I figure, 'nothing ventured, nothing gained.' The application asks for samples of my architectural work, but since I haven't done any, I submit samples of some architectural drawings I have constructed in my company and also photographs of some of my paintings.

I am as much of a late comer to art as I had been to classical music. It had started in a most peculiar way that seems almost too impossible to be true, but it is exactly how it happened.  One of the couples that Sheila and I socialize with most is Marty and Joyce Benson, who are close friends of my cousin Dave and his wife Betty.  Both of the husbands are high school teachers- Dave in English and Marty in art. Besides liking to play charades, we also all like to drink. One evening we are all in Dave's basement rec room playing charades while already pretty sloshed.  Marty has to do the Frost poem in which the author is standing by a barn on a snowy evening, and his efforts are so hilarious that we are all rolling around on the floor laughing uncontrollably.

Before our drunkenness takes over, I do learn from Marty earlier that evening that, in addition to teaching art, he also does some painting of his own, but he does it rarely.  I ask him why so rarely and he says,

"Because I paint in oils and the tubes of paint are grossly expensive- too much so for a high school teacher's salary."  I say to him,

"If I buy the paints, will you do a painting for me?"  Marty says

"Sure, you have to go to Kayman's art store in New Haven. I'll give you a list of the colors to buy."

At our next party a month later, I bring Marty one tube each of cadmium red medium, cadmium yellow medium, burnt umber, raw umber, cobalt blue, cerulean blue, mars black and titanium white, and two months after that, Marty brings me a painting. It is an abstract painting on a 16 inch by 24 inch canvas, with very pleasing bright colors, but neither Sheila nor I like it. Marty had evidently based it on Custer's Last Stand, so it purports to depict a lot of blood and gore. This is not something that Sheila wants to have hanging on our living room wall, so we put it away in the cellar and it never again sees the light of day.

Having been to the art store to buy Marty's paints, my mind now begins to percolate with the thought, "Why don't I try this myself?" I don't know how to stretch a canvas, so I get a load of the same colors I had purchased for Marty, plus some brushes and a painting knife, and begin to try smearing colors around on masonite boards in my basement to see if I can achieve an effect that I like. At this point, my younger son Tommy is 3 years old. One evening while I am smearing paint colors around on a masonite board with a knife, I notice that Tommy, who is in the basement with me, is putting water on the wheel of his upside-down tricycle using one of my spread paintbrushes. I ask him in a curious voice,

"Tommy , what are you doing? "

"I'm painting with this broom."

I go through a lot of trial and error, mostly error, over the next couple of years, sometimes scraping a load of brown paint off the board into the waste can in disgust. Nevertheless, I continue to try painting, and eventually I end up with an abstract design that I am satisfied with, so I let it dry and hang it up on our living room wall. Then I do some more, and start getting some positive feedback from friends including our close friend Cecelia, who is herself an amateur painter. Cecelia and I begin to share our work with several other local painters, and pretty soon the eight of us decide to form a new artists' group in our town.

We start to have summer shows on snow fence around our village center, and I even sell some of my work. This motivates me to try to get some art instruction, so I enroll in an evening adult education painting class. By this time Cecelia has taught me how to stretch a canvas, so I am working on canvas rather than masonite, except for some constructions on plywood that marry pieces of driftwood with small areas of jig-sawed sections of wood wrapped in brightly painted canvas.

One of these constructions wins best-in-show at a juried art show that takes place in our local Arts Consortium. Eleanor Lundgren, who is one of our painting group, far more skilled than I am, and whose husband is a well-known architect, has submitted a very accomplished impressionist painting of a group of women wearing colorful clothes evocative of Vouillard that is rejected by the jury. At the show, she looks at my prize-winning construction and tells me sardonically,

"You will probably sell that in New York for $80,000."

Of course, nothing of the sort ever happens.

The first night of class, I show up with a thirty six inch by forty eight inch canvas and I am the only male in the class. All of the housewives in the class have brought tiny canvasses measuring no more than 18" in any dimension. We are charged with producing a still life with a vase and some flowers and fruit. While I am certainly no Matisse, I do prove to be able to work in a representational manner, and the fact that I have been working big has helped me to loosen up and create some free-flowing line. I proceed then to take a number of drawing and painting courses at the arts workshop in New Haven. As a result, by the time I have to furnish samples of my art work as part of my application to architecture school, I am able to include some representational pieces along with the abstracts.

A month after my interview with one of the faculty, and the submission of my application materials, lo and behold, apparently because the admittance committee is composed of a lot of very liberal, free thinkers, and the time of my application happens to coincide with all the ferment around Yale and many other campuses involving student and faculty opposition to the Vietnam war, I am able to welcome Sheila home from work with the fabulous news,

"Sheila, can you believe it, I've been accepted at Yale!"

We are both thrilled and begin to dance around the kitchen.

"This means that I can follow my dream while we remain in our existing home and the kids remain in their existing schools."

Sheila is as thrilled as I am that this has become possible. Her support of my trying to fulfill my dream merely cements us together more completely, despite my endless philandering, of which Sheila is only too well aware, although she doesn't learn the whole story until years later.

She has known from the beginning that I am a ladies' man, and that I don't seem to be able to resist the enticing flirtations of any female who is admiring my physical appearance. Despite understanding and expecting it, she is deeply hurt when I end up in bed with yet another voracious female. She says,

"Grady, if you really love me, how can you have sex with other women?"

"Sheila, my giving in to one of these women has nothing to do with my loving you.  They are two different, unrelated things."

Of course anyone who knows anything about women knows that this is a very hard sell. In fact, most women would hear this as a complete self-serving crock of shit.

Still, all the things that join Sheila and me together have so far outweighed my continuing difficulties with other women, and her strong, unconditional support of my career switch certainly adds mightily to the strength of the things that we share.

And so I begin my architectural education as a full-time first-year architecture student at Yale School of Architecture. The admissions committee is evidently intrigued by the idea of a building contractor with artistic aspirations trying to become an architect.

Most of my classmates are fifteen years younger than I am, and I right away notice a vast difference in student attitudes from when I was in college the first time.  Then the students displayed a high degree of deference to the professors, no matter what they might privately think of them.  Now, though, it appears that the students give almost no deference to the knowledge, education and experience of their teachers.  I am shocked that my classmates talk back to the professors as though they are just other students. Most of the professors are well-equipped to deal with this disrespect. The structural engineering class we all take is taught by Harvey Fisher, a nationally –known structural engineer who practices in New Haven, and who had worked on the design and construction of the Empire State Building. I can tell that Professor Fisher has long experience because he lectures from old sheets of papers that are yellowed and curled at the edges, looking as though he had used them for decades, as evidently he had.

Professor Fisher is a great man, with tons of practical experience, but he is not one of these pompous professors who thinks that his shit is ice cream, and he doesn't mind the aggressive attitude of his students. In fact he is challenged by it, probably because he is so knowledgeable, experienced and quick-witted that he can easily handle any student's point or question, no matter how far out.

He shows his creative and flexible thinking when he describes to the students during one class that, in investigating conditions on a particular job for which his firm was doing a forensic investigation, he found on the job some metal that was so thin it could be characterized as "reinforced paint". I greatly admire Professor Fisher's resourcefulness in using creative humor as a way to engage his students.

Perhaps standing as a metaphor for the whole changed environment of higher education that I am now experiencing is the fact that, carved right into the wood on the front side of the lectern that Professor Fisher and other professors are using are the following words, "Richard Nixon is not a motherfucker," and I am amazed to see this prominent irreverent graffiti remain in place during the entire period of my matriculation at Yale.   In my first college days, the administration would never have allowed such graffiti to remain in place even overnight, never mind for several years, as happens at Yale School of Architecture.

Other graffiti emblematic of the changed times is the graffiti in bathroom stalls, which in my first stint at college would have consisted mostly of crude drawings of penises and breasts, the stuff of common pornography.  Now, while sitting on the toilet, I am looking at witty graffiti such as "look down, and down", and then "Now up and up", and somewhat better drawings of women having babies, with the exhortation to the men that this is what their preoccupation with sex leads to. This graffiti is a result of the fact that the women students don't confine themselves to the use of the women's bathrooms on alternate floors`, yet another tell-tale difference from back in the day.

More whimsical, yet another example of how much has changed in less than two decades,  is the fact that, carved right into the sheetrock walls by the telephone on the wall of the hallway just inside the door from the outside are these complete song lyrics:

"You must remember this, a kiss is just a kiss, a sigh is just a sigh, the fundamental things apply, as time goes by. Moonlight and love songs never out of date, hearts full of passion, jealousy and hate, woman needs man and man must have his mate that no one can deny. It's still the same old story, a fight for love and glory, a case of do or die. The world will always welcome lovers as time goes by."

I get a very large charge out of seeing this nostalgic graffiti, because it is at one and the same time an illustration of my fellow students' lack of self-control and disrespect for school authority and school property, but at the same time it is also an appreciation of pop cultural history that I share. The remarkable thing I notice on this second time around higher education is how young people can on the one hand be so into new ways of thinking, ever newer technology, and new ways of behaving, and yet still be so old-fashioned! Many of the women like to wear vintage clothes. I think of the thing my father always used to say,

"The more things change, the more they remain the same!"

I get into a pattern during my first year back in school. I start off the day at the intermediate school my company has under construction on the way into New Haven. The union employees I employ there, masons and carpenters, cannot believe that I am going to architecture school. They consider architects to be effete, probably homosexual, picture painters that know nothing about construction. These grizzled construction workers with decades of construction experience have zero respect for architects and little more for engineers (they have probably never worked on one of Harvey Fisher's jobs.) I tell them,

"Well, I don't know what most architects know about construction, but this is going to be one architect who does know how to build a building!"

One day at Christmas time, I take my younger son Tommy to the jobsite for the workers' Christmas party, when Tommy is still about three years old. The men all get a big kick out of seeing Tommy in my arms and pay him a lot of attention. John Lombardi, the carpenter foreman, teases Tommy,

"Where's your hard hat?"

Tommy puts his hand over his heart, obviously thinking that John has asked him where his heart is at. I'm not sure that John and the others even realize what Tommy's gesture means, or understand how it is a response to John's teasing question.

Since my first morning class doesn't start until 9:00 a.m., I have time on the way to school every morning to visit my intermediate school job. At lunchtime and again after my afternoon classes, I have time to check in at my office to keep track of the projects we have underway and are bidding for future work.  Although I had worried that I would be very stressed for time in trying to maintain a working life while at the same time attending graduate school, this turns out not to be a problem.  I find to my surprise that I can manage my time much more effectively and efficiently than my 22-year old classmates.  I do find that I am putting a lot of mileage on my 1964 Chevy Nova, so I wonder when I will finally beat that car into the ground.

The fact that I, unlike my friends, am once again a student, does not prevent Sheila and me from enjoying our normal social life.  On a warm June evening, we are attending an evening party with 25 or 30 other people at the suburban home of my friend, Dan Ametrano, who is a plumbing contractor and one of my steady subs.  The Ametranos are very social people with a wide circle of friends, so Sheila and I don't know about half of the people at the party.  The party begins with swimming in the Ametranos' outdoor in-ground pool.  After everyone has changed back into their street clothes and are all sitting around in the living room enjoying cocktails, I become aware that a cigarette is waving around in front of my face. I then realize that the hand holding the cigarette is a slim, feminine hand attached to a slim, feminine arm, and that the arm belongs to a very attractive brunette. When she finally has my attention, she says,

"Hi, my name is Jane Hershey, what's yours?  I saw you at

the pool and thought we should meet."

"I'm Grady Markell."

We then begin a friendly conversation in which Jane informs me that she is married to a Yale physician who is not at this party.

She says,

"My husband is so busy that I never see him, and I am dying for some action. You could be part of that."

I am a bit taken aback by such boldness, but I do not get up and walk away or say anything to discourage Jane's forwardness.

I tell her,

" I am also very busy, in particular because I have enrolled at the architecture school while still working in my construction business. I don't have a lot of time to spare either."

Jane expresses amazement that a college-educated businessman in his mid-thirties is now going back to graduate school in architecture, and at Yale, no less.

Jane says, "But you do have to take time out for lunch every day, don't you? Why don't we meet for lunch some day and we can get to know each other a little better."

I am reluctant to get involved with someone new, given how busy my life is and that I am happily married to Sheila, plus it is evident that a relationship with Jane will be a continuing involvement, not just a one night stand like Laurel, but after all, and against my better judgment, I can't help but be flattered by such fervent attention from a beautiful woman, so I take Jane's phone number and promise to call her sometime soon to arrange a lunch date.

Two weeks later, I come into school and find a note on top of the drawings on my desk under the sharpener for my drawing leads. The note is written in a sweeping feminine hand on a perfumed piece of note paper. The note says,

"Grady, why haven't you called me? I am waiting with 'bated breath to hear from you."

The note is signed simply: "J".

So, intrigued, I go ahead and call her, saying

"You remember the guy you waived a cigarette at in the Amatranos' living room? Hi, it's Grady".

Jane enthusiastically says,

"Hi, it's terrific to hear from you. Let's have lunch tomorrow."

"How did you know where my desk was to leave your note?"

"C'mon, I know my way around the university. You forget that my husband is a doctor at Yale. I just went to the architecture school offices and learned where the first-year class was setup. Then I just had to ask one of your classmates which was your desk."

So I say, "Where would you like to meet for lunch?" and she says,

"There's a great place called Fitzpatrick's near the architecture school where they serve drinks and deli sandwiches piled high with meat. Let's meet there tomorrow at 12:30".

"OK, that will give me time to make my 2:00 class. I'll see you there."

At 12.30 the next day, I am standing around at the entrance to Fitzpatrick's waiting for Jane. At around 12:35, I spot her coming up the sidewalk wearing a dark blue suit and frilly white blouse, looking quite vivacious in dark, curly hair. We greet each other warmly and proceed inside the barn-like restaurant, where we are seated upstairs in a booth on a mezzanine level. It turns out that Jane is an art history major, so we are able to share a lot about art and architecture.

Jane says, "I'm very impressed that you decided in your mid-thirties to go into such a challenging field without the usual drawing experience."

"Well, I have done a lot of oil painting and some pencil drawing, so I'm not a complete neophyte with respect to drawing."

Jane asks, " what prompted your decision to apply to Yale Architecture School?

I was naturally expecting that question, so I say,

"Are you familiar with the TWA terminal building at JFK airport in New York?"

Jane says, "No, I'm not aware of it."

This surprises me that such a well-educated sophisticated person would not be familiar with Saarinen's TWA building.

"The next time you are going to fly anywhere, arrange to fly on TWA and leave from New York. You'll see what I mean. There is no way I could explain it to you without photographs, which I don't happen to have with me. The fact is that the architecture of that building completely blew me away, and firmed up a vague idea I had been germinating in my mind as an amateur artist that I wanted to get into something creative, where I could be responsible for giving form to the projects that I am working on."

Jane is obviously excited to be with such a dynamic person as I appear to be.

She says,

"So, you're even more than you appear to be in a bathing suit!"

" What do you mean by that, what are you talking about?"

Jane says flirtatiously,

" Let's leave that till later when you visit me at my house some evening."

So we finish our last beers and head out to the sidewalk. I tell Jane,

"I have my car, can I drop you anywhere?  Jane says,

"Sure, that would be very convenient.  My car is over a couple of blocks."

She gets into the front seat, and I reach my arm from behind her to give her a seductive squeeze, but instead my arm inadvertently brushes across her hair and knocks her wig askew.  This is a complete shock to me;  I haven't had the slightest inkling that her very attractive dark, curly hair is not her own.  I bring my arm back where it belongs and say nothing about it to Jane, nor does she say anything while fixing her wig back in place.  We both pretend that this has not happened, but both know that, because of it, I will not be calling her to arrange a cozy evening tete-a-tete at her house while her husband is working late.

# CHAPTER THREE


# ARCHITECTURE

I have graduated from Yale School of Architecture with a Master of Architecture degree, but there are no jobs in architecture firms in Connecticut due to the recession. This prevents me from becoming legally registered as an Architect at this time, because Connecticut state law provides that no one can take the state exams to be registered as an architect without first apprenticing with a registered Architect for two years.   By the time I graduate from Yale, I have had to turn over the construction company to Bob Raster, my principal assistant.  I had been able to hold on to the company for the first two and a-half years of school, but in the final semesters, my school work load for the design seminars has become too intense to do satisfactorily other than full time.

So, after graduation, being so familiar with the construction process, I start to design and build houses on spec. It is not necessary to be a registered architect to design houses in Connecticut containing less than 5000 square feet. Because I have been stimulated while attending architecture school by seeing formations and structures occurring in the natural environment, I think of the house walls as being merely the separation between the interior and the exterior, not as forms in and of themselves.  The natural world is mostly not composed of rectangles, but rather of continuous curves of perception.  I want people inside the houses I have designed for them to perceive the world outside as a continuing sequence, not broken up into boxes by arbitrary corners.

The world is a sphere, and it revolves around the sun in an elliptical orbit. This causes the sun to appear to travel across the sky over and to one side of the house in a continuous curved line from the eastern to the western horizon. Therefore, I feel that the dividing wall between the inside and outside should be a curve, not a straight line. Since I am building in wood and not steel or plastic, and I must build economically because I'm doing it on spec, this means that the wall cannot be a true curve, but it can be segmented in straight sections forming an overall arc. To the extent that people do see my houses as objects, I want them to see a curved form more naturally occurring in nature, just as Saarinan's fabulous TWA building appears to be a bird with wings spread, about to take flight.

I build my first house, to be occupied by Sheila and me and our two boys, right on top of a curved granite ledge outcrop. While I was an architecture student, I had noticed the open lot surrounding the ledge outcrop while on the way down to the shorefront park in town. From the southeast side of this outcrop, there is a view of the water. The north and east sides provide open views of the salt marsh.

Accordingly, my first house, to be built on this granite ledge, is a unique design consisting of a series of rectangular bedrooms stepping up the rise from the west side to an open-plan curved living/kitchen/ dining area on top of the rock. The living space is divided between an open lower area and a mezzanine above just the inside of the space, leaving a two-story wall of glass on the east and southeast sides, and making the inside part of the living area under the mezzanine, surrounding a large granite fireplace, feel like a snug, warm cave on the inside of the open area with the views through the wall of glass.

Several years later, during the northeast power blackout for several days, Sheila and I and the boys are all lying in our sleeping bags in front of a roaring wood fire in this fireplace, looking out at the outer portion of the living room with its wall of glass to the starry sky outside. I actually feel like we are the early humans shown in their caves with their eyes glowing in the dark in the first part of "2001, a Space Odyssey".

The structural support for the central portion of the house is to be provided by a twelve-inch diameter concrete column wrapped in the same pink Stony Creek granite that the house is sitting on, and surrounded with granite-faced fireplaces on both the lower and upper level.

One warm spring day, I am on the rock outcrop to start the construction. I am working alone, because the task at hand can be performed by one man. The first task is to drill four holes into the granite, each one a full twelve inches deep, to accommodate the four one-inch diameter vertical steel rebars that will provide the reinforcing for the concrete column in the center of the house. When I had first contemplated in advance this drilling into very hard granite rock, I had expected that it would require very hard and continuing effort on my part. Much to my surprise, the rented electric-powered rock drill pushes the steel bit right down into the granite like a knife through butter. This gives me a feeling of being muscular and powerful like Howard Roark drilling in the rock quarry in "The Fountainhead".

Because the concrete foundation has to be built directly on the irregular rock surface, and because I know that therefore the foundation will be completely exposed on the outside, I do not want to first build level concrete footings on the rock and then form the walls on top of the footings, as is normally done, because that will expose the rough footing edges on the outside and will present an ugly scene. Because I will therefore not have level footings upon which to form the concrete foundation walls, I cannot use the standard pre-manufactured wall panels normally used by concrete contractors to build the foundation. I will have to make my own plywood wall forming panels, cutting them on the bottom with a jigsaw to fit the profile of the rock. The wall panels will then be secured with the double two by four walers at the top and bottom of the walls, which are connected through the plywood panels with steel wall ties, secured on the outside of the walers with steel so-called "dogs", which secure the panels in place and can be knocked off with a hammer after the concrete has cured. Except for jig-sawing the bottom edges of the panels to fit the rock, this is the standard way our construction company has been building concrete foundation walls for its school jobs.

One of the carpenters my company had been using for years to build these concrete forms is Manny Delouise. The thing about Manny is that, not only is he a good carpenter, but he is a raging drunk, a very sloppy-looking guy who is actually drunk during the work day. When I am about to get started with the foundation, I meet Manny at the site to show him the ropes for this job. Sheila happens to be there at the same time as Manny because she is delivering my lunch to the site, so I introduce Manny to my wife. Sheila, being the polite woman that she is, manages to hide her horror at Manny's appearance and to speak to him in a friendly, open manner.

At home that night, Sheila says,

"Grade, are you actually going to hire **that** man? I can't believe you would actually hire and pay such a slobby drunk!"

"Well, babe, actually I am hiring Manny because, although he is admittedly a terrible drunk, and is in fact usually drunk while he is working, the truth is that, despite his alcoholism, he is an excellent carpenter and very familiar with the method I am using to form the concrete foundation walls. So, yes, I am hiring that man and will pay him at the end of each week."

Sheila remains extremely skeptical but doesn't say any more about it. She is obviously not going to argue with me about how I am building our house.

With this foundation, though, I have invented a method never seen by Manny before. I want the exposed foundation walls to look like the stone cuts on highways, so I nail pieces of driftwood onto the inside faces of the wall panels and add a red powder to the concrete trucks while they're mixing the load before they pour, which results in a rough, reddish wall rather than the typical smooth grey concrete foundation wall.

One of the contractors working on the house later, obviously not understanding what I am trying to achieve, says to me, upon seeing the finished foundation wall,

"Well, at least you can hide it with bushes", which is not actually possible, because the house is surrounded by exposed solid granite ledge.

Because the foundation is stepped over many levels, has a twelve foot tall concrete column in the center, and is on a site inaccessible to concrete trucks around most of its perimeter, the concrete has to be pumped through a hose rather than simply flowing down the chute from the truck by gravity. I have the help of Manny and Bob Raster, to make the big pour, which requires 6 trucks of 12 yards each and takes half a day.

After six months of very hard work, I complete my first house, and Sheila and the boys move in and are very comfortable and happy there.  It turns out that in Tommy's bedroom, there is a small unexpected bit of elevated floor space high in one corner, resulting from some unplanned alignment of the roof rafters relative to the bedroom walls.  I am able to turn that anomaly into a serendipity by installing a wood ladder on the wall to give Tommy access to this little piece of elevated floor in the corner, and Tommy has the imagination to make frequent use of his little hideaway in the corner of his bedroom.

It is summertime and Sheila and I are enjoying some warm, muggy weather.  We are very happy together.  Our oldest boy Wally is in high school and the younger one Tommy is still in grade school.  I am working hard in my design/build efforts on spec houses, being outside most of the time on jobsites.  Because I do a lot of the physical work myself, I have developed a muscular physique and usually sport a great tan.  Sheila works part time doing secretarial work for a retired college professor who lives in a modern house down by the water.  She can drive there in less than twenty minutes, and can enjoy a relaxed atmosphere in a shoreline setting with a great view of Long Island Sound, working for an old, distinguished and very well-educated guy who can't remember anything, and who is extremely appreciative of Sheila's organized and efficient mind.

Sheila also enjoys Mr. Harrison's wife, Cynthia, who comes from money and is a very elegant, well-educated and sophisticated woman, and who also has a well-organized mind like Sheila.  Cynthia is well aware of her husband's failing memory, so she sympathizes completely with Sheila's constant struggle to keep her husband focused.  The two women frequently enjoy with the Professor something you might call a "high tea" together in the afternoon.  Cynthia pours.

One day, Sheila calls me at work to tell me that her Subaru hatchback won't start, and she is trapped at Professor

Harrison's house.  I remind her,

"Don't you remember that we have AAA road coverage? All you have to do is call the emergency number and they will be out there within an hour."  Sheila says,

" OK, Grade, great, thanks for the reminder.  I'll do that."

After work that day, I notice that the rear end of Sheila's hatchback is dented in.

"What happened?"  Sheila tells me  in an exasperated tone of voice,

"While I was waiting for AAA, Mr. Harrison thought he could help me get started by giving me a push with his car, but, can you believe it?,  as I'm waiting for the push,  I look in the rearview mirror and see him coming toward me at some considerable speed.  He didn't pull his car up to mine before accelerating, but instead he started from several feet back and simply drove into my car, which jolted me sitting in the driver's seat, failed to start my car, and put a dent in the rear bumper.  I told him

'Thanks for trying to help, but I'll wait for the AAA serviceman.'

When his wife, Cynthia,  came outside to see what had made the crashing noise and I told her what had happened, she said to me,

'Charles shouldn't be allowed to do anything'."

Sheila and I are pretty active socially that summer, attending a number of lawn parties with many of the same Christian Republicans we always seem to end up being with at parties in our WASP town. At one of these parties, I notice a new couple- an attractive guy and his pretty blonde wife. I go over to them and say

"Hi, I'm Grady. Are you guys new in town?" The husband right away puts out his hand and says,

"Yeah, my name is Mike Minter, and this is my wife, Gen. We just bought a house over on Millpond Road".

After meeting his firm handshake, I lightly shake hands with Gen. She is open, relaxed and friendly, and gives me a warm smile without being in the least bit flirtatious.

Mike and I for some reason quickly get into a discussion about the religion and politics of our social group. I proudly tell Mike,

"Actually, I've been an atheist since I was 10." Mike responds with great excitement,

"Yeah, me too! It's a pleasure to know that there are other atheists around besides me. What made you decide that you are an atheist?"

"Well, I said, the first thing was that the illustrations of

Christ and his disciples in Palestine or whatever it was called in those days that we were shown in Sunday School looked so foreign and far away. I couldn't connect these images of people in robes in the desert with my own life in the twentieth century. It probably didn't help that our Sunday School teacher always had excess mucus in the corners of his mouth while he was explaining Bible events to us- it was pretty disgusting. Later on, it struck me that so-called 'acts of god', which people call calamities such as hurricanes, tornadoes and earthquakes, are all natural events well understood by scientists. Later I heard a lecture by Julian Huxley and that convinced me that I was truly an atheist. How about you?"

Mike says,

" I realized that almost all of our current knowledge about the world and ourselves has been learned in just the past couple of hundred years. Contrary to what people believed 2000 years ago, we now know that the universe is over 13 billion years old, that planet earth is about 4 billion years old, and that life has existed here in some form for over 3 billion years, during most of which time it existed only in the form of microscopic organisms such as bacteria, fungi and algae. It's long past time when we should bring our beliefs into line with scientific knowledge, instead of continuing to believe in the stories of Genesis."

When I call Sheila over to meet the Minters, we all hit it off immediately. Within a few short weeks, we are sharing evenings together, having supper at one house or the other. We soon become best friends. As against our two sons, the Minters have four, and all of their first names start with the letter "C".

Sheila and I have never owned a boat, but every once in a while we enjoy a ride in someone else's. Two of our friends, the Emersons and the Fairchilds, own sailboats, and we have been out on Long Island Sound a couple of times in those boats. The Minters own a Boston Whaler, which is a fairly stodgy motor boat that rides high in the water, but it is roomy enough to accommodate two families. That summer Sheila and I take a more extensive boat ride with the Minters all the way across the Sound to a beach on Long Island.

We bring both of our kids along, and the Minters have two of their sons. The eight of us are comfortably accommodated in the Boston Whaler, and it is a gorgeous, warm summer day. As we get out onto the water, I take my shirt off and enjoy the warm day in just my bathing suit. At that point, I get into a rather personal conversation with Gen, who is wearing an attractive bikini, which shows her modest, partially exposed bosom. She starts to tell me about her experiences of having other guys flirt with her, and as she is telling me this, I am aware of how good Gen's body looks in her bikini, and I can readily understand why guys might hit on her. For the first time, I see Gen as a sexually-desirable female.

We all enjoy a great time on the beach, including a great lunch of ham and tuna sandwiches, fresh peaches, soda and beer, and a pan of delicious brownies that Gen made. We don't start back until very late in the afternoon, and not only is dark approaching, but now the weather starts to turn. A cloud bank comes across from the West and the wind begins to pick up. After we are underway, the rain starts, and I scramble to help Mike pull the frame and cover over the boat so that we won't get completely soaked. As the rain and wind start up and then intensify, the boat begins to toss and turn, because the Boston Whaler is a very shallow boat that just rides on top of the water. This gets everyone really scared. Getting wet is now the least of our worries; now we are beginning to worry about getting back to the Connecticut shore.

The wind and pounding rain, and the violent tossing around of the boat, continues for a half hour to an hour or more, and we all are huddling and holding each other under the flimsy boat cover and shaking in our boots. Fortunately, Mike is able to keep the motor running and at last we make it into safe harbor and everything calms down. We all breathe an immense sigh of relief. It is sobering for us to realize that our trip across the sound has turned out to be very risky and almost costs us- not only our own lives- but that of our children.

A month or two later, still in very warm and muggy weather, I go over to the Minters' house in the afternoon to look at the back of the house where the Minters have decided to build a deck. Mike outlined his intent several weeks earlier, but now I need to take measurements and photographs so as to design a deck that fits their house. Mike, not seeing any reason why he has to be there, naively stays at work and leaves Gen to be the one to show me the area and to help me as needed with the measurements.

Much to my surprise, Gen is again wearing the same bikini she had on when we went to the Long Island beach in the Boston Whaler a few weeks earlier. I say to her,

"Boy is it hot!", and she says,

"Feel free to take your shirt off", so I do.

No sooner am I shirtless than she says,

"We need something to cool off, let's have a gin and tonic."

I don't normally drink alcohol before the sun is over the yardarm, but it is hot and her offer is tempting, so I give in and join her in a drink. In the course of moving around together in the same small kitchen to make the drinks and collect some munchies we begin to bump into each other accidently or on purpose, and then, without even any flirting, we are suddenly in a tight embrace kissing for all we are worth. Gen takes my hand to pull me into her bedroom.

I say,

" We shouldn't be doing this",  but Gen says,

"Of course we shouldn't be doing this, but I know perfectly well that Mike has been fooling around even though he denies it, and now I'm determined to enjoy something I want."

Within a flash, her body is no longer protected by the bikini, and I can see that she is a true blonde.  She helps me remove my pants and, when she sees my full nakedness and at the same time is fully aware of my reluctance to do what we are about to do, she says,

"You don't know what you have."

I don't know what she really means by this statement, but I don't ask for an explanation.  I am not sure whether she just means that my cock is bigger than her husband's or whether she means something more, but we proceed to carry the scene to its logical conclusion, while her words stick in my mind for me to chew over in the future.  As our bodies blend together with my climax, Gen says,

" That is what I call 'niceness'. "

Although there turn out to be a couple of more social occasions between the Markells and  Minters after they build their deck,  when Gen and I sneak a kiss in the other room, during which she says to me:

"Your kisses really turn me on",

I never again go to bed with her. I don't know whether Gen ever brags to Mike about our afternoon tryst while arguing about his running around, but, apparently not, because Mike never comes after me about it, and if Sheila suspects that something may have taken place between Gen and me, she doesn't show it. In any case, the Minters cease to be our steady friends, and in fact, like so many of our other friends, the Minters end up getting a divorce only a couple of years later.

It is a very hot August and we and the boys are at our usual housekeeping summer cottage behind Nauset Beach on Cape Cod.  We have been going to this beach ever since our honeymoon, when we were able to occupy a small, rustic cottage right on top of the dune.  We could walk out our front door and run straight down the dune to the ocean.  Those old cottages have since been torn down because of the establishment of the National Seashore by the Federal Government, which required demolition of all the cottages close to the dunes after they were no longer owned by the same family.

The cottage we have been renting since then is set back several hundred yards from the ocean, so we have a short walk to get to the beach.  Nevertheless, we can clearly hear the surf from our cottage, especially when we are enjoying lunch or cocktails on our roof deck, which is accessible only from an outside staircase.  This particular summer we decide to try a different beach just for the change of scene, so we go up to Truro to the Head-of-the-Meadows beach, which is about 35 miles north of the beach we usually use.  Actually, this outer shore of Cape Cod is all one long beach extending from Provincetown down to Chatham.  The different sections of this long beach, each with a different name, are accessed from different side roads off the Mid-Cape highway.  When the four of us get down to the Head-of-the-Meadows beach, we find it almost completely deserted, despite the fact that it is a beautiful sunny morning, but I do notice a couple of young women in bikinis about 100 yards down the beach to the south from where we are going to set up. Even from that distance, I can tell that they are stacked. I am surprised to observe that they seem to be watching us at least as intently as I am watching them

Sheila and I are both amazed when, only a few minutes after our arrival, these pretty young largely-exposed women appear on the beach right where we are. These girls are right in front of us saying "Hi" through their broad smiles. It is as though the soprano and the mezzo have miraculously come down from the stage from the fourth act quartet in Rigoletto, each losing 30 years and 30 pounds while changing from evening dresses into bikinis and then magically appearing on the beach in front of us. Their bikinis leave very little to the imagination and the décolletage is equally impressive.

After these awkward, pointless greetings to and from complete strangers, we pay no more attention to the bikini-clad girls, Sheila and I simply settle into our beach chairs and the boys run down toward the water to build a sand fort, all as though these girls were not there, which indeed immediately becomes the fact, as the stacked girls head back to the spot from whence they came. They appear and then disappear with equal suddenness. It's like the scene in the Wizard of Oz when Dorothy is visited by Glinda, the beautiful blonde witch of the north, who, after a brief conversation, just as suddenly leaves, and Dorothy says,

"People sure do come and go quickly here."

Sheila and I are both dumbfounded by this awkward intrusion, and can't figure out what is motivating the young women. Sheila says,

"Maybe they're prostitutes."

"That's doubtful. They don't look a bit like prostitutes, other than the obvious display of flesh. To me they look like well-endowed young women who are doing a good job of filling out the skimpy current styles in bathing suits."

I'm thinking that if they are prostitutes, how in the world could they expect to accomplish anything by accosting a man who is on the beach with his wife and kids? Did they expect me to suddenly abandon my family and come up and roll around with them in the dunes? Sheila says,

" But if that's the case, why did they come over to us?"

"Beats the hell out of me, I haven't a clue."

The following fall I have one of my spec houses on the market.  One day I get a call from Lois Bullard, a local realtor I know.  Lois says,

"I have a couple from New York who I would like to bring to your spec house on Cattail road.  They are interested in a "contemp."

This shorthand by Lois for a contemporary- styled house grates on my ears because it sounds like "contempt,"  but I have enough sense not to say anything about that to Lois.  The husband is a New York City shrink named Jason Haverson, who surprisingly is not Jewish, although his wife, Dahlia, is.  During their visit to this spec house, Lois compares it to my first house that I had built for my own family but which has recently sold, so the Haversons then want to see that house.  I call the new owners and they agree to permit the visit.

The new owners are a pair of local doctors, both husband and wife, who are very nice  and do not act like privileged people.  Amazingly enough, they had been looking for a traditional colonial home but were shown my very modern house because their realtor knew that they wanted a home with lots of light.  That was a realtor who literally thought outside the box, because from the standpoint of architectural style, you couldn't hope to find two houses more different than a traditional colonial and my first open-plan modern house.  The Haversons are very impressed with my first house, but not more so than Jason's amazement upon seeing the doctors' two vehicles in the driveway. He can't get over the fact that more than one vehicle in one residence driveway sports MD plates.

Nevertheless, after the Haversons buy a lot in a nearby up-scale subdivision which contains many contemporary homes, they begin to work with me to design a house for them on their lot. During the design process, which extends over several months, the Haversons invite Sheila and me to visit their New York apartment for dinner. We take the railroad to the city, and I am hauling with me the large, cardboard model of the house I am designing for the Haversons for their Connecticut lot. They live in a building containing about 25 floors in the 30's in midtown Manhattan. Sheila and I take a taxi from Grand Central.

The Haversons' apartment occupies one entire floor of the building, and it's exterior walls on three sides are all glass. Dahlia can stand at her kitchen sink and look out upon the Empire State Building only a couple of blocks away. At the time of our visit, Dahlia is pregnant with the Haversons' first child. She is wearing a tee shirt that reads "Construction Below". Sheila and I are both immensely impressed with the Haversons' apartment, if not necessarily with the couple themselves. Nevertheless, everything is cordial between us, and I am glad that they seem to be in basic agreement with my design. I leave the model with them so that they will have time to look over the design at their leisure.

The house I have designed for the Haversons is all on one level, except for a few steps between the different areas of the house, so as to accommodate the building to the gently sloping site. It's general shape is in the form of a butterfly, with a living area 'wing' and a bedroom 'wing' containing four bedrooms. The center of the house, both functionally and structurally, is a small central hexagon, the six points of which are columns supporting the radial laminated beams which in turn support the roof. The central hexagon functions as the centrally- situated foyer, and features a skylight which lets natural light pour down into the center of the house.

Before construction begins, I am personally involved in clearing some trees from the site, and one very hot day I am working with a chain saw with my shirt off when I see the Haversons drive into the property to check on progress. I notice that Dahlia is looking at me from the passenger seat, so I give her a wave. From that point on, I have the vague sense that Dahlia, who has now given birth to a son, begins to flirt with me in ways that are so subtle that I never explicitly notice. I probably don't notice because I don't see her as a desirable female, but just as my client. While the house is under construction, she is sometimes there without Jason, because the Haversons have rented a summer home on the water nearby so that they can keep track of construction progress.

One winter day, I drive there with the Haversons  because they want to show me the interior relationship of the kitchen to the living area of their rented summer home.   As I arrive at the site, I realize that, because the ground is frozen and slippery, and the house is considerably lower than the road, we should leave our cars by the road and walk down to the house. Jason stops his Porsche next to the drivers' window in my old Chevy truck and asks me,

"Why are you stopping at the road?"

I say,   "The ground is frozen and very slick. If you drive down there, you'll never be able to drive back up."

Dr. Haverson, the New York psychiatrist, in his typical self-assured manner, says,

"Oh, I'm sure I'll have no problem."

I later smile to myself upon hearing from Jake,  my excavation contractor, that he had to take his backhoe down to this summer home later that weekend and drag Dr. Haverson's Porsche back up the slippery slope with a cable. Only much later am I able to perceive that slippery slope as a perfect metaphor for my relationship with the Haversons.

During the work week, while Jason is working in New York, Dahlia frequently comes to the jobsite to see how things are going.  One day, as my two helpers and I are working on construction of the walls, Dahlia is carrying her baby son with her in a sling around her neck.  She says to me,

"Isn't he cute?"

I mumble a vaguely positive response, but in fact, to my eyes, the baby bears a remarkable resemblance to Lou Costello.

The Haversons start to get impatient with the progress of construction, and learn that at the same time as I am working on building their home, I have another building project in town, down by the water.  That project involves moving a small commercial structure back on the lot to permit construction of a new foundation resistant to flooding, re-setting the structure back onto the new foundation, and then adding a couple of new wings to make a larger office.

I try to assure the Haversons ,

"Don't worry, I have a separate crew working on this office building, it is not causing any delay in the construction of your house.  Whenever I go to the office site, my work crew at your house has been given full instructions to proceed with the work as expeditiously as possible. I am on your site every day to maintain progress."

Nevertheless, they are getting impatient.  They really have no idea about how houses are built or how long they take, especially one with such a unique design as their house, and they have an expectation of instant gratification. They go so far as to repeatedly drive by my office project to check on whether I am spending a lot of time there.

Interestingly, from that office project on the shoreline there is an excellent view across the harbor to a modern house which has been recently designed and built by the architect Tony Mara for his own family. From the vantage point of my office building, Mara's house looks like a sixty degree-thirty degree triangle, standing on the short side.

On another day when Dahlia comes to their house under construction, she is standing with me in the living room area, where the ceiling slopes up to a wall of glass, similar to the living area ceiling at my first house that the Haversons had seen. Dahlia asks me,

" How high was the ceiling at your first house at the glass wall?"

"It was 24 feet at the highest point." Dahlia then asks me,

" How high is our ceiling at the glass wall?"

"It is approximately 22 ft. high." She says,

" Jason is very upset by the fact that this living room is not as high as the one in your first house." I point out to her,

"the dimensions of this house are shown on the drawings which you approved. The dimensions of my first house have nothing to do with it."

Remarkably, while this conversation is going on, Dahlia keeps suggestively moving her hip against me, each time with me moving a little away so that her body is no longer touching mine. This is just like the episode with Gloria Hanson a decade earlier, except with hips instead of tits doing the pressing. I am completely amazed by what Dahlia is doing, because I have been mostly unaware of any past flirting on her part, and these moves seem to be coming out of the blue.

They are also confusing, because she is pressing against me while at the same time delivering complaints about my design. After a few minutes, Dahlia stops moving against me.

Only a few days later, I am served with legal papers claiming that I have breached my agreement with the Haversons, and they are seeking $250,000 damages. As soon as I read through the legal complaint, I realize what has precipitated it- it was my failure to respond to Dahlia's advances. I gain a renewed respect for the truth of old adages- Hell does in fact have no fury to match that of a woman scorned, especially if she is Jewish. Actually, Jews are the same as everyone else, only more so.

Because the Haversons are alleging breaches of the agreement to construct the house as designed, the case quickly falls apart because I am not only the contractor but also the architect who created the design. The lawyers representing the Haversons, evidently not being familiar with a situation where the architect on the project is also the builder, have pleaded a case that doesn't fit the facts.

Curiously, the person who presents me with a proposed settlement to end the case is not an attorney but none other than Tony Mara, the architect who designed the 60-30 house across the water. From this, I realize that Mara has been engaged by the Haversons to replace me as their architect, and I deduce that they must have been impressed by Mara's house as seen from my office building while going down there to check on me.

Mara is not looking for any money on the Haversons behalf, he just wants to end my architectural services so that the coast is clear for him to become the Haversons' architect to complete the house. He knows that it would be a breach of professional ethics for him to start working on a project where there is already an architect of record.

We negotiate an arrangement allowing Tony to replace me as their architect. I wonder how Dr. Haverson would react if he knew that what had actually caused him to bring this suit was not that I had done anything wrong in the design and construction of his house, but rather that his wife had a hidden agenda, and that I didn't acquiesce in his wife's desire that I fuck her. I wonder if he later gets cuckolded by anyone else. Some years later, I learn that Tony is also fired by the

Haversons before the house is completed, I'm reasonably sure for reasons having nothing to do with climbing into Dahlia's bed since Mara is a short stocky older guy without any evident sex appeal.

I have been successful in designing and building several modern houses, and getting them sold, but I am not making much money.  Somehow the cost of land, subcontractors, employed labor and financing costs eats up most of my profit.  I joke about the fact that I do all the work while the bankers and realtors sit on their asses and make all the money, which is not that much of an exaggeration, and is certainly no joke.  Sheila does not complain, even though our economic needs continue to require her to work.

While the kids are in school, she is able to earn money from her secretarial job with Professor Harrison, which she actually enjoys.  We are both in very good physical shape, me from the physical work outside, and her from her cast-iron constitution and from her active, healthy lifestyle. She almost never gets sick, which doesn't surprise me because I have been impressed by the photo of her grandparents' generation of siblings in their eighties sitting in an arc of chairs in their living room, with their feet planted firmly on the floor.  I can see with my own eyes the solid genes that my wife carries.

I begin to look for other ways to supplement our income, and consider trying to do some modeling. I know that I am considered to be handsome, especially by women, and I figure that maybe I could put that to use, so I sit for some poses with our excellent family photographer, all of the poses in a business suit, shirt and tie.  I take these photos to New York and get in line at an ad agency.  It is a unique and interesting experience for me, and I get a kick out of it.  Because I am in good physical shape and have no hair loss, even from any receding hair line, I do not feel out of place.  One time at Kennedy airport while I am waiting for our niece to arrive from Georgia, I walk into a waiting area full of middle aged guys and one of them asks me,

"Would you sell me your hair?"

I am in my late forties but really could pass for early thirties.  This is a cliché in personal ads, but in my case it is actually true.  In the agency waiting room, while waiting to be seen by the man doing the initial evaluation of applicants, I look around at the others waiting- both boys and girls mostly in their teens or twenties.  I feel that most of them are no better looking than I am in my forties, but I do spot a couple of drop-dead gorgeous teenage girls.

When my turn finally comes after waiting about an hour, the man, who is about my own age, asks to see my photographs and then studies them with some care and attention.  After a few minutes he tells me,

" I need my  own photographer to take some different pictures. Here is a name and address down on 14th street. You'll have to make your own appointment for pictures and will have to bear the cost."

While wondering if this ad agency only serves as a business

originator for the photographer, I nevertheless make the appointment for the following week and again take the train to New York to meet with the agency's photographer.

The photographer is on the third floor, but the building has an elevator to reach all the upper floors, so I don't have to use the stairs.  The building is not like the high class, high-rise buildings in midtown, but it is not totally grubby either.  The elevator is self-operating, and gets me to the third floor with no trouble. I ring the bell at the photographer's door, and am greeted by a young man in his twenties, wearing khakis and a hunting shirt, who lives in a spacious apartment with plenty of natural light from windows to the street. He asks,

Modelling shot of Grady in workclothes

"Are you Grady Markell?"

After confiming who I am, the photographer spends about 45 minutes with me, taking a series of shots of me in a business suit, with or without a raincoat, and one shot wearing work clothes and pretending to use a skill saw to cut a board.

The photographer never suggests any shots of me in a bathing suit, or in underwear, or even with just my shirt off. I am also so clueless about myself as to not suggest any such poses either. Although I wait weeks for some response from the ad agency, I never receive anything in the way of further appointments with that or any other agency, and so I give up on the idea of trying to develop an auxiliary modeling career.

I have completed my tenth spec house, designed and built on a hill surrounded by open land protected by the Land Trust, which enjoys a distant view of the Sound and also of the church steeple in the center of town. The house has a rectangular section containing bedrooms, joined to an entry-kitchen-dining-living space in the form of a spiraling conch shell, with the roof of that area supported by a series of large laminated beams resting on the masonry fireplaces in the center, and becoming ever longer and higher as they spiral from the entryway around through the kitchen, then the dining area, then the living space. I am showing this house to a middle-aged married couple from the other side of New

Haven, who are brought by Barbara Rusk, a large, buxom blonde real estate agent with an aggressive manner. They seem to like the house, but there is something reserved about them, as though they are not really interested in living in my town.

My intuition about this couple is borne out a few days later when I get a phone call from Barbara Rusk. She explains to me,

" My client, Garrison Colmer, was impressed with how you sited your house on the top of that hill. He owns a large parcel with an old house on the top of a hill in Woodbridge. He would like you to take a look at his house and tell him whether something can be done with it. Are you willing?"

I ask her, "Is this guy for real?"

"He is definitely for real. He owns a company upstate and has a ton of money. He is also one of the nicest guys I know".

"OK, then, sure, I'll come over and take a look at it."

A week later, I drive over to Woodbridge and find myself on a typical suburban road with very well-maintained, middle class three-bedroom ranches and split levels on very well-landscaped one-acre lots, with the houses set back 75 feet or so from the road. When I come to the street number given me by Barbara Rusk, I see a pair of stone pillars with a driveway between them curving around to the right in an uphill direction, similar to my spec house that the Colmers had looked at. Driving up a fairly steeply-sloped drive through woods, I arrive at the top, where a 150-year old large Victorian pile is located. I meet Gary Colmer there and we walk through the house. The house is in extremely worn-out condition and obviously needs a lot of work.

I say to Gary,

"I don't understand what you are interested in here. You admire my modern house with large, open spaces inside and now here you are showing me this old Victorian house all chopped up into small rooms. To try to renovate this house into a modern, open space interior would mean spending a ton of money in a futile attempt to make a silk purse out of a sow's ear. Extensive renovation work typically costs more than new construction. It would be far more sensible for you to design and build a new modern house on this lot. There are plenty of possible locations." Gary says,

"You're probably right. Would you be interested in working with me to design a new house on this property?"

"Of course I'm interested, that is what I do."

The next day, I call Barbara Rusk and tell her about my meeting with Gary Colmer. I tell her I have agreed to work on the design of a new unique modern house on Gary's 8-acre lot.

"Thanks very much for introducing me to the Colmers. This looks like an excellent project where I can really do my thing!"

Barbara is very cordial and says,

"Well, I was also very impressed with the house you showed us. I happen to live on another street quite near Gary's property and would like to show you my own issue with the entry to our existing house. Would you be interested in looking at it? I tell her,

"Sure, I can do projects of any size and complexity."

I never turn down work, no matter how large or small the construction. I know that it's going to take months of working with the Colmers to design their house, so in the meantime I can tackle Barbara Rusk's smaller project. We make a date to meet a few days later. I hang up the phone and exult to myself,

"Wow, one showing of my spec house and now I've got two projects on the other side of New Haven!"

I meet with Barbara and her husband, Frank, to talk about their issue. They have a large colonial which is high on their lot, with a driveway leading up to the garage on the right side, and a front entry accessible only by a winding walkway from the driveway around the front close to the house, where the front door opens directly into the living room. What Barbara wants is a foyer accessible directly from the street in front, where guests typically park. I will have to deal only with Barbara. As is typically true of married couples that I deal with, Frank, the husband, is only interested in the cost. The design decisions are made by the wife. It only takes me a few days to design a sky-lit entryway, to be reached by a curving set of stone steps up from the street. Within two weeks after Barbara approves the design and Frank agrees to the price, I start work constructing the steps and entryway.

I had been warned by one of my architecture school professors about dealing with married couples designing a house. He said that you have to be careful to elicit input from both husband and wife. There is a danger that the process of designing and building a new home might actually cause the split-up of the marriage. This happens because, when just buying an existing home, the couple simply accepts the layout of the house they see as already existing. When designing a home from scratch, the architect elicits from the couple, and each one individually, how they actually want to live. This may expose the fact that they have different ideas about how they actually want to live.

I had seen this concept proven some months earlier, when I had no sooner read a glowing newspaper article about this couple that had just designed and built their first magnificent new home after being married for many years, than I heard that they were divorced and the house was on the market. Now when I talk to couples during the design process, I am acutely aware of this danger. The red flags go up when the wife is trying to tell me something about what she wants certain parts of the house to be like, and the husband hushes her up.

It is now September, with beautiful warm and reasonably dry weather. I am working with a small crew on Barb's project. One morning just before coffee break time, my crew and I are working on her front steps. Because of the weather, I and my men are working with our shirts off. After a while, I become aware that the warm summer air is infused with perfume, and at first I can't locate the source. But then I realize that the perfume smell is wafting from Barb's bathroom off to the right of the entryway we are building in the center of the front façade and drifting down to where we are working.

After smelling the perfume for a half hour or so, I hear Barb calling to me from the front door, like Odysseus being called by the sirens in the Odyssey. I go up the steps under construction and meet her at the front door. Right away I notice that Barb is acting extremely nervous. With a tenuous, wavering grip, she is holding a brochure of door styles for me to review with her. As we are leaning over a little towards each other to jointly peruse the brochure in her hands, I suddenly realize that she is wearing a diaphanous, see-through blouse and that her large breasts are bouncing around under the transparent cloth in plain view.

I instantly understand that the prime purpose of this contrived meeting at the front door is not to look at door styles but to let me know that Barb has a more urgent and immediate interest which trumps her interest in the new entryway I have designed and am in the process of building for her. I perceive that her more immediate interest is in her own private entryway to which she would like to introduce my own private erection.

I do not share in the least Barb's immediate interest. In the first place, she is not my type. To me, she is more of an Amazon, a large, big-boned blonde who is more intimidating than enticing. I tend to like feisty, spirited women, but ones who are petite in body type. Like most men, I appreciate a beautiful pair of tits, but not the big, bulging, fleshy kind that are now being shown to me and which used to be prominently featured in Titter magazine when I was young. Furthermore, I can't forget about Barb's husband, Frank, who is a big man. The last thing I need is to seriously provoke his animosity.

Although it is difficult for me to completely ignore the jiggling boobs right in front of my face, I proceed to do exactly that. I do not shut the door against the view of my helpers, put my hands on her breasts and press my mouth to hers, as she is hoping and maybe even assuming I will do. Rather, I manage to pretend that her large orbs are not in plain sight but are encased in a normal blouse, and to concentrate on the door types we are looking at in the brochure. I have no intention of carrying through on anything personal with Barb, and I do not want to embarrass her any more than necessary, so I act as though I haven't noticed her nakedness. I note the door style she seems to prefer, agree to provide that one in the final design, and then turn around and return to my work, just as though she were normally clothed and this little provocation had never occurred, and I make no mention of it to my men.

I do spend some time after this event reflecting on what happened, since it is unique in my personal experience, and I do wonder what provoked this literally revealing gesture on Barb's part. I do remember an extremely hot day a short time before the day of Barb's exposure when Barb and I were driving around the area looking at similar entryways on other houses. On that earlier hot day, I had removed my shirt because of the extreme heat while we were travelling around. At the time, I had thought little of it and had not been aware of any reaction to my shirtlessness on Barb's part, although, being as sensitive to women's feelings as I am, I did have the sense in thinking about it later that I might have been a little provocative, in that we were not in bathing suits at a swimming pool but were traveling around the streets of the neighborhood.

Now, though, I wonder whether that earlier day had

played any part in her exposing herself to me?  After all, I had shown her my nipples, so why not the reverse?  Could that have been the logic in Barb's mind?   Just another version of you show me yours and I'll show you mine?  This seems unconvincing to me, though, because, for my whole life it has been considered normal for men to appear in public swimming areas topless, while the same is definitely considered verboten for women, except on dedicated nude beaches.   Even little girls who have not yet developed breasts typically wear tops on their bathing suits, but there is nothing unusual about men baring their chests and their little male nipples in public.

When I tell Sheila that night about what happened with Barbara Rusk, she says,

"I can't  believe that a respectable client can be so foolishly brazen!"

"Yeah,  I couldn't believe it either.  I literally couldn't believe what I was looking at."  Sheila marvels that a self-respecting woman can be so aggressive and so heedless about her own embarrassment.

"Still, you have to admire her relative subtlety, in the sense that, even while seductively exposing herself, she did in fact keep all her clothes on, thereby preserving her deniability.  In fact, she did succeed in being able to deny it because I also denied it!"

Yet from that point forward with Sheila and me, "Barbie" Rusk becomes a one-woman cliché for forwardness, recklessness and brazenness.  As for Barb and me, we just proceed on with our construction project as though nothing has happened, thus firmly establishing Barb's deniability.

A little footnote to this strange project is that, the following winter, long after that project has been completed, I get a call from Barbara on a bitterly cold and clear New Year's day.  She says,

"Grady, the entryway roof leaked last night."

"How can that be, it didn't rain or snow last night! Has it leaked before?"

"No, it hasn't, but there was water coming down from the entryway ceiling last night during our New Year's Eve party. We had about 40 people in the house."

"That must have been condensation, not leaking, but I'll come over and check it out tomorrow."

I was not surprised the next day when I removed a couple of suspended ceiling tiles to see that the metal flange around the foyer skylight had not been adequately protected by insulation from the warm, moist air on the inside of the house.  I knew that when the extremely warm, moist air during a large holiday party came into contact with the cold metal of the skylight frame on a frigid winter night, water would naturally condense out of the inside air and drip on the floor. There is nothing wrong with the roof. I proceed to install more insulation around the skylight and put back the ceiling tiles in the suspended ceiling, and that ends the problem. I'm not surprised by this event because I am familiar with the standard problem of water from moist interior air condensing on cold surfaces, which is typically taken by uninformed clients to be a water leak from the outside.

One day I get a phone call from a woman in Westport, who says she has seen my website for architectural services, that she and her husband are considering how they can renovate their hilltop home to achieve their objectives, and that they would like to talk with me about possibly engaging me to assist them in that effort. She has focused on the fact that my website prominently features a number of modern homes situated on elevated sites, which is of particular interest to her and her husband because their home is a modern home in a subdivision of modern homes built since World War II, and furthermore it is located on the top of a hill. We make arrangements to meet at their house 4 days later, in the evening, since she has a day job. I agree to meet them with no strings attached for an initial meeting as I always do. Usually these meetings lead to a job, so I have no problem in meeting without any pay or any contract.

Driving into their subdivision, I am surprised by the fact that all the homes are modern, even though many of them are extremely modest.  Their house is at the end of the road, elevated considerably above it.  Theirs is an ample contemporary home with the living space on the second floor, reached by a steep set of stairs from the small foyer.  She greets me at the top of the stairs and introduces herself,

"Hi , I'm Leila, and obviously you are Grady Markell."

"Yeah, this is me, glad to meet you.".

Leila says,

" Meet my husband Kano",

and again I am surprised to see that he is Japanese, although I shouldn't be because I know that his surname is Miura.

More surprising still is the fact that he appears to be about 20 years her senior.  As for Leila, she is a petite brunette bearing a resemblance to one of Sheila's and my friends, Marion Emerson,  who likes me and flirts with me, and I think "Uh, oh, here we go again!",  but she doesn't have Marion's dark Italian eyes and is not being the least bit flirtatious.  They tell me they have been married for 7 years but have no children. She speaks very softly and deliberately and tends to purse her lips as she says certain words.  I am gratified that she and Kano both participate fully in the conversation as they explain how they want to renovate their home, so I don'thave the worry based on my architecture professor that this process could be destructive of their marriage.

They even have a set of schematic plans already drawn by another architect, but they are not happy with her concept. Their primary goals are to expand their master bedroom area, to get more usable other bedrooms, and to somehow elevate their living area a few feet so as to take advantage of what would be a spectacular view of the Sound. One major problem is that their house is built into the hill such that the ground on the side away from the road is one full level higher than the ground at the entrance on the road side. Also it is apparent that the foundation built into the hill is not adequately waterproofed, because the lower level is so damp as to be almost uninhabitable. On the other hand, their living room where we have our conversation is separated from the kitchen area by a huge stone fireplace and is naturally lighted by large windows on two sides which give the room a very cozy feeling while also looking out toward the water on two sides. The downside of this best room in the house is that a nearby unattractive pinkish box of a house is very close on the corner of the room between the views of the water.

We agree that I will work with their existing plans to see whether they can be tweaked to accomplish their goals and that I will charge them an hourly rate with an upset total fee.

I get back on the highway in a state of exhilaration to have a nice new commission, but I rather quickly come to the conclusion that the Miuras' goals cannot be reasonably accomplished by renovating their existing home. There first of all is the fact that the upper floor will have to be raised three or four feet to truly capture the water views from all the rooms on the southeast side. In addition there is the damp lower level which cannot be effectively dried from the inside-one would have to move the house to permit proper insulation and waterproofing and installation of a perimeter drain on the outside of the foundation wall. In addition, there is very little room on the lot to park any cars because the grade drops off so precipitously. A satisfactory design would have to be based on a two or three-car garage tucked in under the lowest level of the house.

A week later I return to the Miuras with the bad news. I am relieved to find out that they are amenable to a whole new house because they understand completely my reasoning, and would love to have their upper level high enough to enjoy the spectacular water view, would love to have a fully habitable dry lower level and would love to have room to park their cars and those of a few guests, not only in the garage but on the property in front of the house. Also it turns out that they would love to have a Japanese style wet room, where the showers are part of one large room where they can relax in just towels. So I am commissioned to proceed with a full design for a new home on the site.

Two weeks later when I return with some plans, Leila greets me with a rather prolonged hug, which starts to set off some alarm bells. Though Kano is standing right there as she does it, he doesn't seem to notice anything untoward, so I also pretend it is nothing and we proceed to meet and discuss the plans. Since I am even older than Kano, I can't believe that Leila really wants to get down and dirty with me, but I reflect on the fact that she has married someone at least 20 years older than she is and begin to wonder if she has some sort of father complex. This time they make it clear that they will have some problems affording the new house. She has a pretty good corporate job, but he is a day trader working from home, and has undependable income. Kano explains that he intends to act as his own contractor. I say,

" This would normally be a very problematical proposition because owners are usually clueless about all the things it takes to be a successful contractor. But, since you can be on site all the time, and I have so much construction experience, this could work if you engage me to do a much more complete administration of the project than an architect usually provides. I can help you a lot to be a successful general contractor."

They both look very pleased by this, so we set out to do the project.

One very curious thing that happens at this meeting is that Leila shows me a table full of bottles with various colored liquids in them that evidently are some form of medicines or potions that they are trying in an effort to get her pregnant. I have no idea what is in the bottles or how they can possibly have anything to do with her getting pregnant but I don't say anything because I am embarrassed. I think to myself,

"All you need to get pregnant is to sleep with a guy with a good sperm count",

even though I have no idea whether her problem getting pregnant has to do with Kano or with her.

After several meetings with Kano & Leila, I have progressed through a number of design concepts. Initially, I have a main floor plan with a large stone fireplace between the kitchen/dining and living spaces, which continues the layout of their original house, with such a pleasant living area which is cozy while also having lots of glass to overlook the water views. But the proximity of the pink house between the two water views, one to the sound and the other to a pond on the southeast side, kept grating on me until I finally have the epiphany, while coming up the entrance ramp onto I-95 on the way back home, that I can block that pink house by locating the fireplace at the corner looking out onto that house. This is the insight which leads to the final design of the great open living space, in which the corner fireplace is flanked by two huge laminated beams which cut across thespace diagonally and support the whole roof, including a higher area between the beams which contains clerestory glass on one side.

After demolition of their existing home, which is a bit painful for all of us, them for obvious reasons, and even me because I hate to have to tear down that wonderful living room, we get into the concrete phase. I am able to introduce them to a concrete guy I had used on some of my own houses, and to be on site with them while they are forming the footings. I happen to be on the job one very hot morning with Kano with my shirt off when Leila stops by on her way to work. This time she gives me a very warm, prolonged hug and I notice that Kano gives us a charged look out of the corner of his eye. This time I get the strong feeling that I could be the next father figure headed toward Leila's bed, and I hate the thought that this would begin to be a barrier between Kano and me.

Two months later we have completed the first floor decking and are framing the second floor walls and getting ready for the laminated beams to support the roof. Kano informs me,

"My mother in Japan has had what I hope is a very mild stroke and I've got to take a few days off to go over and be with her." I assure him,

"Don't worry, Kano, I can take care of things while you're gone. Too bad you'll miss seeing the crane installing the laminated beams."  He says,

" Leila can't get off work to come with me so she will  be here to answer any questions."

In the evening on the following day I get a call from Leila. She says,

"Grady, will you please come over tonight to help me pick out a design for the front door?"

She and Kano have rented a house nearby to the site for the duration of the construction, and that is where she wants me to meet her.

"Isn't Kano in Japan?"

"Yes, but he won't mind you and I choosing the design for the front door."

I'm thinking of Barbara Rusk's large breasts jiggling behind her diaphanous blouse and wondering, why is it always the design of the front door?  Instead of 'behind the green door it's 'behind the front door'.  Realizing that the front door is once again the opening into something else, I say,

"I don't feel comfortable visiting you at your house without Kano being there."

There ensues a long moment of silence, as though at a service for a deceased person. She evidently has concluded from our extended hugs over the past two years that I am just as interested in getting into her bed as she is in having me there, so my statement has struck her dumb. She murmurs something unintelligible and hangs up.

The truth is that Kano's absence is not the only reason for my reluctance. I am attracted to Leila, and frankly flattered by the attentions of someone twenty years younger than I am, and I really would love to be with her intimately, but I hate to spend an evening away from Sheila and to endure the guilt of being in bed with yet another woman. Sheila and I have gotten onto a very solid basis, with both of us thinking that my philandering is all in the past. I hate to jeopardize all that we have accomplished in getting me focused on our marriage, which is where my heart is really focused. Just like little Tommy on the jobsite that long-ago Christmas, I do sincerely know where my heart is at, the question is, how do I fend off all these women who keep coming on to me?

The very next day, I am on the Miura job to be sure that the framers have the structure ready to receive installation of the laminated beams. I have just arrived and am still standing out in front of the house when Leila comes striding up the hill, absolutely dressed to kill. She is wearing a sharp hat, has full makeup and sports a beautiful sleek pale olive green spring leather coat and spike heels. She looks like she's stepping onto the runway. I've never seen her look more sexy and desirable and I say,

"Good morning, Leila."

Not only does she not give me the usual warm hug, she doesn't even greet me at all or acknowledge that I have spoken to her, as though I am not even there. She simply strides deliberately right by me without speaking one word or even looking at me. I am instantly hurt at such a provocative snub, but I quickly realize that I am looking at the very personification of a furious woman scorned.

I don't want to have strained relations with her for the rest of the job, plus I really would like to get into bed with her, especially after seeing her this morning dressed to the nines. I track her down on the other side of the house where she is meeting with the landscaper. She wants to plan her plantings even while we are still framing the house. She continues to ignore me for a time while talking with Hector, but eventually I am able to speak privately with her.

"Leila, I'm sorry, I didn't mean to hurt your feelings. I don't think Kano will mind my coming over to your place tonight to make necessary decisions about doors." She instantly flashes me a brilliant smile and says,

"Don't worry, Grady, I won't be possessive about you."

That evening I drive down to their rented house which I had seen from the outside but had never been inside. It is above a store and looks like something out of the 19th century. Just in case I need it, I bring a blue pill with me. I ring the bell, and as soon as she opens the door she hugs me tight for several minutes and then looks at me with hungry eyes. I kiss her and she responds fully, so we kiss deeply for several minutes and then I remove my coat and we head back toward the bedroom without even bothering to go through the motions of looking at door brochures. I tell her,

" I need to use the facility" but don't tell her it is so I can use the sink to take the blue pill. I come out into their bedroom and we begin to kiss again, with open mouths and busy tongues. Their bedroom is quite large and has a queen size bed and a row of closets with louvered doors down one whole side of the room. When she takes off her blouse and brassiere, I see that she has very small breasts, but not a boy's chest like Laurel. This doesn't phase me- it just means there is nothing to get in the way.

When I get naked and climb into bed with her, I say,

"I feel guilty about doing this with you while Kano is away."

She says, "Well, you certainly wouldn't be doing it if he were here. Don't worry, what he doesn't know won't hurt him, and he won't know, you can be sure of that!"

The way she says this gives me the perverse idea that maybe he actually does know.  Maybe that whole story about his ill mother in Japan was a false cover story, and he is actually here hiding in the closet where he can watch his wife enjoying another man's cock.  I am aware that there is such a thing as a husband who actually gets off on being cuckolded by his wife as he watches her with her lover.  Of course I don't mention such an idea to her because for one thing I doubt verymuch that such could really be the situation.  As I enter her she begins to moan with pleasure as her vaginal muscles gently but firmly squeeze me.

"Grady, this feels so wonderful, I've been longing for this for quite a while, actually ever since I ran into you shirtless that morning on the job.

"Story of my life", I say. "I love being inside you also."

Her moans increase in intensity as she says,

" Give me what I need, Grady, I really want all that you have."

I get the fleeting idea that I am also hearing moans from the closet, but this is certainly just my imagination.  The pleasure reaches an intense crescendo as I climax with full force inside of her and she is ecstatic as she realizes happily that I have expended a full load of sperm into her deepest center.

"Oh, Grady, I love you for giving of yourself so completely!"

We continue to lie there for ten minutes or so as we continue to kiss and caress each other while I'm still inside her. Then I remember all the colored bottles on the table a few months earlier and I get the distinct impression that this is all she wants from me and that I will not be faced with continuing pressure from her to be with her in the future. I don't know how I know this, but maybe it isn't only women who have intuition.

After that, everything returns to normal on the job and Kano is back after a few days to report that his mother's stroke was very mild and that she has not been significantly diminished. He seems exhilarated to be back with Leila and I get the strong feeling on many mornings that he has been making love to her a lot since his return. When I see her two months later she seems to be in bloom, which makes me suspect that she has actually finally become pregnant. Since they have been married for over seven years without getting pregnant, I imagine that it must have been my one night with Leila that most likely made her so, but nothing is ever mentioned by either of us, and in the meantime Kano and Leila seem to be thrilled with each other.

Three months later the new house is substantially complete so that Kano and Leila can move in, and at that point they confirm to me with great excitement that in fact Leila is pregnant, and she even begins to show.  Leila says,

"Grady, we want to meet your wife and show her the house, can you get her down here soon for dinner?".

"Sure, I can bring her down, when do you want to do it?"

"How about a week from Saturday, say around 7:00 p.m.?"

"I'll make sure Sheila has no conflict with that and let you know tomorrow."

Sheila is perfectly willing to come to the Miura's house because she wants to see another example of my work and she is a little curious to meet Kano and Leila after all I have reported to her, which of course has not included my evening in the sack with Leila.

"You know, Grade, I am a little nervous about Leila because of your telling me about how she is always hugging you suggestively every time you meet."

"Don't worry, babe, Leila is finally pregnant after all these years with Kano, so she is completely involved with her husband and is in fact thrilled to be with him. You can be completely relaxed."

When Sheila visits the Miura house, everything is friendly and relaxed and she relates well to both Kano and Leila. Sheila is duly impressed with the open plan house design with the large beams soaring up to the fireplace in the corner, and doesn't observe any hugging between me and Leila.

At the same time, in my head I am thinking about being inside Leila that one night and begin to secretly worry that Leila will give birth to a baby who has no Japanese features. From this point on, I spend six months dreading the appearance of a newborn baby who doesn't look the least bit Japanese.

When the new baby is born, I am intensely worried about seeing it, because I know it won't bear any resemblance to Kano or to those Japanese pilots I saw in the movies during the war, and I have the fear that, since the baby will have no Japanese features whatsoever, the jig will be up about Leila and me. This will be intensely painful, because I have enjoyed my relationship with Kano during the job every bit as much as with Leila, leaving aside the sex on that one night. I don't want to hurt Kano. It would be just so horrible to introduce any doubts in Kano's mind just at the moment of his supreme happiness and pride with his new son.

As I enter the hospital, I feel like a fish out of water and entertain the idea of just taking off and disappearing, but I have always persevered throughout my entire life to finish anything I have started. I always show up. I ride up the hospital elevator with fear and loathing in my soul as I approach my moment of truth. As I go down the hall to Leila's room, I hear the murmur of a lot of voices and realize with a shudder that all of the grandparents are there in the room. I dread going into that room.

Entering the room, I first see Leila's beaming face with the baby in her arms, and then Kano standing beside her and smiling fondly at the baby. Around the room are four older people. I recognize Leila's parents right away because I have met them a couple of times before while the house has been under construction, and I shake their hands warmly, murmuring how good it is to see them again. Kano then introduces me to his parents, Mr. and Mrs. Miura, who have come all the way over from Japan to take part in the blessed event. They are a handsome older couple, with unmistakable Japanese features, and they appear to be pleased as punch.

When I bend over to take a closer look at the baby, I realize with intense relief that he looks like any other newborn baby I have ever seen, with a crinkled, reddish, wizened face and crested hair like a tufted titmouse. While I know that this will merely postpone the moment of truth, I still entertain the hope that the lack of Japanese features will never become clear to Kano or his parents, and that, as long as none of my own features are obviously apparent in young Ken, Kano's family will simply come to realize that Ken looks more like his Irish mother.

I say,

"I feel like an intruder to be here taking part in your family's private moment of pleasure in the new baby." Kano says,

"Don't be silly,  Leila and I both consider you to be practically one of our family."

Kano's mom beams at him and almost explodes with pleasure as she tells Kano,

" Son, take a good look at this new baby of yours, he's a dead ringer for his father!"

"Yeah", cries Leila's father enthusiastically, "Baby Ken is a chip off the old block!"  Everyone in the room, especially Leila and me, is wearing a huge grin.

# CHAPTER FOUR


# GOD'S GIFT TO WOMEN

In the late summer of the year that I complete the Miura project, Sheila is informed that Professor Harrison has died, and so that job comes to an end. She is searching around for another job and sees in the classified section that bartenders are needed and that she can take bartender training from a company that specializes in that kind of training. This sounds to her like a new and challenging occupation that would involve her with people, which is her cup of tea.

Sheila takes the training and does very well at it. She knows her way around a kitchen. She interviews for an evening bartending gig at a hotel bar an hour away from our home, and gets the job after that one interview. Sheila begins a regimen of bartending three evenings a week from seven to eleven p.m. The travel is a bit onerous, but the pay is good.

The fact that I have become an architect hasn't changed the Markells' social life. We continue to socialize with the same group of friends we had when I was just a builder. One couple among our group of friends is Daniel and Marion Emerson, who own one of the sailboats in which we occasionally take a ride on the sound. They have been an integral part of our social set in town for many years. Marion is another art history major who also takes a keen interest in architecture. She is a very petite, vivacious brunette with a slim figure and with dark, Italian American features. In fact, I had identified her as having such a background the first time I met her some years ago at a restaurant where our social set was getting together for the first time.  I said to Marion at that time,

"Your facial features suggest to me that you come from a family of people with a Mediterranean area background- perhaps Greek, or Italian."

At that time she said nothing but her husband Dan pooh-poohed this candid observation, because evidently, as a WASP New Englander, he was in denial about his wife's ethnic background since he felt that it would impede his social-climbing ambitions as a doctor among the town's WASP elite.

Now, however, it is a few years later, we are at a party at the Emersons' house, and I am in a private conversation in a corner with Marion.  As an art history major from RISD, she is fascinated with my current architectural projects.  She also shares with me our liberal politics.  We are both Democrats in a Republican town, which also puts her at odds with her husband.  During this conversation, Marion confirms my initial impression upon meeting her, readily acknowledging that her birth family is an Italian-American family named Ciano living in the Providence area.

A week or two after this party, Marion "happens" by the construction site where I am building another spec house.  I am working around the fascia on a ladder and am shirtless on a hot day.  I come down off the ladder and show Marion around the house, which is nearly completed.  Marion acts more flirtatious than she has in the past, and I am flattered by her attention. She has the petite body type that appeals to me and I also find her dark, ethnically- different features very appealing and attractive, especially her deep, dark eyes. I feel pleasure to be in her company and enjoy her observations about my latest project.

A few days later, Marion calls me and says,

"I'd like to come over to your home office and get your advice about a building problem at my house."

Marion's home had been designed by another architect.

"When do you want to come over?" She says,

"How about right now?"

"OK, sure, I can spare some time."

When she arrives at my house, we sit down in my small home office and she spreads some drawings out on the work table. As we peruse the drawings, Marion tries to explain to me what the problem is, but I am having a hard time understanding what she is driving at. In the meantime, she is practically entwining herself around me, and once our faces get close enough together we suddenly begin to kiss. The kissing quickly escalates into practically consuming each other's faces. Before long we are on the rug and taking off our clothes. I see that Marion has a very thin body with small breasts, but with a very thick black bush. When I enter her, I am amazed at the strength of her vaginal muscles, which contract with great power around my member, squeezing me tight. Although I am able to complete the connection, I feel reluctant, almost that I have been hoodwinked into an affair that I don't really want.

After everything calms down, Marion suggests that we take a shower together, which we proceed to do. While in the shower, Marion asks me,

"Are you for real?"

"Of course", I say,

without ascertaining what she means by asking. I don't press her for an explanation, but merely file her question away in my mind. I had never asked Gen either what she was referring to years ago, when she had said, "You don't know what you have."

Of course, I don't share this experience with my wife, and I begin to have problems sexually with her. My guilt is inhibiting my sexual performance with Sheila, which now becomes completely debilitating. One night, I lose my erection just as I am about to enter her, and I sheepishly apologize for having been working too hard lately. Sheila is devastated by this because she knows in her heart of hearts that something more significant must be going on.

Three weeks later, I am with Marion in the bedroom of the

spec house where Marion recently visited the site. The house is on a hill set back far from the road, but slightly visible from there.

We are meeting in the evening, when Marion can get out of her house on some plausible excuse and I have some free time while Sheila is working at her bartending job out of town. We are lying in a sleeping bag on a mattress, because the house is not yet heated and not furnished. We are in only our underwear when we hear steps coming up the entrance ramp to the house, and, within a few seconds, Sheila bursts into the room. She is surprised and yet not surprised to see me there with Marion, who immediately is on her feet confronting Sheila while wearing only her panties.

Sheila starts to cry while at the same time she is yelling at Marion and me. She shouts through her tears,

"Tonight I quit my job because I felt uneasy being so far away from home and I was suspicious of what the mouse might be up to while the cat's away. While I'm driving by here, I see the light on in Grady's spec house, which shouldn't be on, so I come up to investigate and now, what do I find but my husband almost naked with some whore!" Marion says,

"You have to know that Grady and I share a lot in common and have really taken to one another." Sheila is riled up even more by this statement, shouting at me,

"I'm working my ass off in a hotel 50 miles away from home to put bread on our table, and what are you doing?, you're messing around with one of our friend's wives."

I am impressed by the fact that Marion, standing her ground with her exposed small breasts and only her panties on, has the chutzpah to say to Sheila,

"But you don't **own** him!"

Sheila makes no response to this outrageous yet legally accurate remark, but simply glares at Marion and strides out of the house.

Of course this scene has the effect of pouring a pail of cold water on my romantic adventure with Marion, so we simply get dressed while saying very little, and we both leave. Sheila's strongly heartfelt and justifiable outburst is too tough an act to follow.

That night, Sheila and I have an intense and extended conversation.  Sheila asks,

"How long have you been fucking her?"

"This was only going to be the second time; we did it a few weeks ago."

"I'll bet that was why you couldn't get it up with me last time."

"I don't know how this happened with Marion. She came over to the spec house a few weeks ago and then one thingjust led to another. I don't feel like it was really my intention."

I don't mention the very intense kissing I did with Marion nor her powerful vaginal muscles. Sheila says,

"Boy, what a load of crap! Do you love her?"

"No, you're the one I love."

"You sure have a strange way of showing it!".

"I'm very, very sorry. I want to end this and make it right with you."

"Who else have you been fucking? Let's get everything out on the table. I want to know about every woman you've ever been with."

I say, almost with relief,

"OK, I'll start from the beginning. You already know about Julie in grade school and bloodless Donna in high school, but I never had sex with either of them nor with any of the other girls I dated briefly.

In college, I never told you about Sam, who was a friend of my fraternity brother Joe Macleod."

I proceed to tell her about that afternoon episode.

"That was never repeated, principally because I didn't enjoy it.  I also never told you about that little southern dancer that worked as a receptionist in the construction company.  She was a nymphomaniac, and I couldn't resist going to a motel room with her one evening.  I'm not saying that I was not willing, but because of her nature our relationship moved into serious territory without much initiative on my part."

I proceeded to relate the extraordinary circumstance of Laurel's flat-as-a-pancake chest and about having oral sex with her.

"We were never together after that."

As I am giving this peroration, I am paying close attention to Sheila to gauge her reactions so far. I feel that my most recent affair with Marion is the most serious of my sexual affairs with women other than Sheila, so I feel confident that my recitation of past transgressions will at least not make the situation I am in now any worse.  Sheila does express surprise about the sex with Sam, since that was before we were married and I had never mentioned it, but she does not interrupt me or tell me to stop, so I continue.

"I told you about those times when a woman would come on to me completely without my encouragement or consent, like Gloria Hanson, the Professor's wife, and that realtor, Barbara Rusk.

Along the same lines, you remember when you and I were at the town beach one hot day last summer? I never told you that the young woman on a nearby blanket kept looking over at me while miming fellatio with her popsicle. I couldn't believe what I was seeing, that she would do that in plain sight on a public family beach, yet there was absolutely nothing ambiguous about it. I was tempted to find out who she was, but then I did nothing about it.

Of course you know about Dahlia Haverson, and that nothing happened there either. If it had, maybe I would not have ended up getting sued, but could have gotten into a whole lot worse trouble.

You remember that party we went to at the Ametranos in Orange a few years ago when I was in architecture school? I don't know if you met or even noticed this woman named Jane Hershey who was at that party. While we were all just sitting around the living room, she started waving her cigarette around in front of me to get my attention, and then we had a conversation about my going back to school, etc. Her husband is a doctor at Yale who was not at the party, and she was hot to trot for some extra curricular activity- she made no bones about it. It was so blatant that I was intrigued enough to have lunch with her at Fizpatrick's one day.

Fortunately, we had this embarrassing but actually comical incident in the car after lunch, when I was going to put my arm around her, but accidently knocked her wig loose, which was a total shock because I was unaware that her attractive hair was not her own. Neither of us acknowledged what had occurred, but that incident was like a douse of cold water on whatever spark may or may not have developed between us, and I never saw her again."

"I believe that there are only two more things I have to tell you, and I apologize profusely if this hurts you. The first one involves our former friends, the Minters. You of course remember the boat trip we took in their Boston Whaler across to Long Island that summer. You may remember that Gen was wearing a scanty bikini, and that she and I got into some intense conversation on the boat, which was really only about the fact that other guys had come on to her in the past but that she had rebuffed them. She was maybe flirting with me a little bit then, but it was pretty subtle."

"Some weeks later, when I go over to their house one afternoon to take measurements and photographs for their deck that I was designing, she tells me that Mike is cheating on her even though he denies it, and that she had wanted to have sex with me ever since that day we went swimming on Long Island. We end up making out and having sex that very day.

I was not interested in continuing it with her although I know she would like to have kept it going, so that ended up being the only time, although we did some kissing at later times when you and Mike were elsewhere in her house. I know that this one is probably particularly hurtful to you since we continued to have social events with Mike and Gen for some time after that."

Sheila is remarkably calm after everything I have told her, and I feel a sense of relief to be getting it all off my chest. Sheila seems to be very glad to finally have me levelling with her, and nothing she has heard is any worse than what she has been imagining anyway. Sheila asks,

"Did Mike ever find out about you and Gen?"

"I don't believe so. Mike never came after me about it.

Sheila, I have one more one-night stand that I have to tell you about, and this will hurt, because it probably had serious results. As you suspected from all the hugging, Leila Miura wanted me. Late in the job, while Kano was away in Japan to see his sick mother, she wanted me to come over one evening to ostensibly pick out a design for the front door- shades of Barbara Rusk. I told her, 'Leila, you and Kano are both my clients. I don't feel comfortable being alone with you at home while he's away.' There was a period of heavy silence on the line before she said goodbye and hung up."

I proceeded to relate to Sheila how Leila snubbed me on the job the following day while dressed to the nines, and how

I relented and made a date to visit her the next night.

"We still had a ways to go on the project and I dreaded completing it while she would remain so angry with me. Also, and this is clearly another self-serving rationale, I figured this would make Kano almost as suspicious as if I actually went to bed with her, so I went there and we had sex the following night. The funny thing is that she seemed to have the specific agenda of getting my sperm in her so that she might get pregnant. I told you about all those colored bottles on her dining room table that time and about how they had been trying to get pregnant for years."

Sheila looked stricken as she said,

"Does that mean you are the real father of their son Kenny?"

"Well, I certainly have no intention of getting DNA tests. Kano and Leila are extremely happy, and so are his parents."

I told her how Kano's mother had reacted in the hospital. Sheila says,

"Well, I am not a bit happy at the idea that you may be the father of someone else's baby, but I must confess that even that is better than you being in love with her. Are you?"

"Babe, you know perfectly well that's not true, and even as for **her** feelings, she has not bothered me since that night and is very happy with her husband and new son."

"Have you told me about all the women?"

"Yes, that's it."

Sheila says,

"This thing with Marion is now the remaining huge problem and it's very serious because she will soon be free. I don't know how you really feel about her, because over the years I have observed you and her at parties in long, intimate conversations, and I know that you are attracted to her. Now I understand that her marriage is ending and that she is on the prowl, so she is therefore a really serious threat."

"Probably true", I say.

Sheila says,

"I have to be very wary of Marion. She is armed and extremely dangerous."

We are quiet for a bit, each carefully watching the other's face. Sheila says,

"Marion is a real threat to us, we've got to do something about it. Do you still love me?"

"Oh, yes, you have to know that I do".

"I have a hard time believing this in view of all that you've been doing.  I couldn't believe the nerve of that bitch standing there in nothing but her panties and telling me that I don't **own** you.

You have to get some help to find out who you really are and what and whom you really want."

"What do you mean, get some help?"

" You need to unburden yourself with a psychiatrist and try to figure out your thing with women."

Sheila may be oversimplifying the situation here based on her own very brief session with a psychiatrist.  Some years ago, she had been feeling guilty because of her negative feelings about certain members of her family so she went to a psychiatrist one and only one time who simply pointed out to her that her feelings were inside of herself and didn't hurt her family members, who didn't even know about her feelings. This is all Sheila needed to hear, and her feelings of guilt simply disappeared.  Sheila has always been a consummately practical person.  She realized that what her family members didn't know wouldn't hurt them or her.

"OK", I said, "I'll definitely  look into this soon."

"You have to do more than that. You have to move out of here and leave me alone for some time while you figure things out.  I don't want to be sleeping with you here while not knowing who you really are, who else you are secretly fucking and who you really want to be with."

This is very painful for me to hear, but I can hardly complain or object because I know that Sheila's pain is far worse than mine and that I have brought all this on myself. Reluctantly I say,

"OK, I understand. I'll move over to the condo for awhile." This statement refers to the fact that, at the same time as I have the spec house for sale where Sheila had her confrontation with Marion and me, I also have under construction a forty two-unit condominium project in Branford, in which I have several unsold units, one of which I can use as a temporary residence.

It is now past 2 a.m. after all of this intense conversation, so we end it and go to bed, although we both take some time to calm down and go to sleep while listening to each other's breathing.

The next morning I sadly move a couple of suitcases of clothes over to unit 11 in the condominium. The units are fairly upscale, with dining area and living space separated by a few steps and just a wide railing, i.e., the living room is sunken with respect to the dining area and therefore has a ten foot ceiling. The view from the living room is through a pair of transom-topped glass doors leading to a deck overlooking the wetland. The dining room is connected to the kitchen by a pass-through and by an octagonal shaped breakfast area which sticks out from the side of the unit.

The units are townhouses, with the bedrooms upstairs. I have been using unit 11 as a sales office, so it has a dining room table and a couple of chairs, a table and three chairs in the breakfast nook, a couch, chair, coffee table and TV in the living room, and some kitchen dishes and  utensils with complete appliances.  Upstairs there is only a large mattress on the floor of the master bedroom but a fully appointed bath and functioning laundry room with washer and dryer.  All-in-all, an adequate bachelor pad.

I'm not used to sleeping alone, especially on only a mattress, and after a few nights when I need several brandies before I can go to sleep, I start to think about how not to be sleeping alone.  I had been fascinated for years with the personal ads in New York Magazine, especially those placed by women.  I had wondered who these women really were and what it would be like to meet them.

As I look through the personal ads in the current New York magazine,  I read one that says

"**Witty Blond-** Psychoanalyst, late 40's, seeks lusty, tall, handsome, successful Renaissance man, 50-59."

This intrigues me because I figure maybe I could accomplish my need for a shrink while at the same time enjoying a relationship with a woman, not a very smart idea, probably, but we men are nothing if not foolish. I am in theright age bracket and had been elected most versatile by my high school classmates, and I knew that I appealed to women, even though not being extremely tall. But I answer the ad, lying that I am divorced, and including a photo of me taken when I was clearing snow from our driveway during the previous winter. The photo is quite striking because the snow is scattered all over my full head of dark hair.

I see another ad reading:

" **Attractive Brazilian Lady**- From Westchester, 45 years old, 5'3",110 lbs. Well-traveled. Loves opera and speaks four languages- Portuguese, Italian, English and Spanish. "

I answer that one too, enclosing the same photograph, and do the same for another ad reading:

"**Fairfield County, CT**- divorced Jewish female, pretty, petite, young-looking 45. Seeking serious relationship with handsome, sincere, upbeat professional. Note and photo a must."

After only a few days, I get letters from all three of these women, and I arrange to meet all of them. The first is the Jewish female, whose name turns out to be Cynthia, whom I arrange to meet at the central fountain in Lincoln Center. I am very familiar with that venue because Sheila and I have been regular patrons of the Metropolitan Opera for over a decade.  A week after hearing from Cynthia, we meet at the fountain and she turns out to be just what her ad indicated, a petite, dark-haired, clearly Jewish woman in her forties, still with youthful looks and exuberance, and she is not disappointed upon meeting me either, so I must appear asshe had expected from my photograph.  We are both grinning at each other and waste no time in getting into animated conversation.  I suggest to her,

"Let's go over to Oneal's and have a drink", which she readily agrees to.

We spend about an hour and a half at the bar, both enjoying a couple of martinis while we discuss a wide range of topics, including national politics (we're both Democrats) current and past movies, our marriage experiences, the arts, my Jewish mother, our kids and even abortion.  As we are leaving Oneal's with a pleasant warm glow, she tells me,

" I have never in my life had a conversation like that with a man." She says,

" Would you like to accompany me to a wedding in Riverdale next month?"

I say, "Sure, that would be fun, is it a Jewish wedding?"

"Absolutely, maybe you can find out more how you feel about your ethnicity." We part with a hug, but our lips only brush lightly.

The meeting with Paula, the Brazilian lady, two weeks later, is a whole different bag. In the first place, because Paula is from Westchester, we meet at the entrance road leading into the Pepsico sculpture garden in Purchase, N.Y., where Sheila and I had visited on numerous occasions. We have some conversation in my car, and then decide to go to a movie in New Rochelle, which is a French-based thriller involving a female hit-person, called "La Femme Nikita".

We are casually comfortable with each other, and after the movie, we decide to have a light supper and some drinks at a nearby pub. Once again she and I enjoy a non-stop conversation on every topic under the sun, but this time, when we get back into my car, we start making out like tall dogs. I don't mean that any clothes come off, but we are doing some intense kissing with our tongues actively engaged. When I get her back to her car at Pepsico, we arrange vaguely to meet again, but it never happens, because, although she is ready, willing and even anxious to take it further, I find no motivation to do so because she is not that attractive to me.

The blond shrink is yet another story. We arrange to meet in Midtown at Grand Central Station, where we have no difficulty spotting one another because we had exchanged the photographs. She is undeniably an impressive looking female and seems happy to meet me. Her blond hair, which looks true, is well set off by an attractive pale green suit with a frilly white blouse. We go down to the oyster bar for drinks and hors d'oeuvres, and again have a vigorous wide-ranging conversation. While there is nothing overt about which we disagree, her body language is cold and controlled. Even her facial expressions seem to be tightly managed. I wonder if the problem is really me, that I don't relate well to blonds, despite my girlfriends Julie and bloodless Donna. After about 45 minutes together, we part on the street by almost simultaneously stating,

"We must do lunch", both grinning because we both know that there is no intention that it will ever happen.

Since the appointment has aborted early, and it is a beautiful warm evening in Manhattan, I decide to take a stroll, just heading down Fifth Avenue, and I end up going all the way to Washington Square and even further into Greenwich Village. Somewhere around 4th Avenue, I stop in at a cozy looking Italian family bar. I'm only one of four or five older guys at the bar, but there is a table by the window with two nice-looking girls in their 30's. Every so often I look around at them and each time I do, I see that they are checking me out. Even though I am a good 15 to 20 years older than they are, I figure, what the hell, nothing ventured, nothing gained, so I stroll over to them and say, with a big smile,

"Mind if I join you?" They both simultaneously say,

"Sure, why don't you? One says,

"My name is Joan, and my friend here is Phyllis, who are you?"

"I'm Grady, how do you do?"  Before we can say much of anything else, the matronly proprietor comes around from behind the bar and says,

 "This is a family place, we don't allow pickups in here. You'll have to leave."  I wisecrack,

 "What do you mean, this is no pickup,  I was a classmate of these girls at Vassar. ( This being at a time when Vassar was still girls only)."

Of course, that wisecrack gains no traction, so I drink up and head out the door.  Just in case these girls are as interested in getting together as I am, I wait outside for a few minutes, and, sure enough, they right away settle up with the bar tender and come outside to meet me.  We head up the street to another bar, and I say,

"That was pretty ridiculous, all she accomplished was to lose three good customers."

The three of us cozy into a booth at the next place and we order drinks and some sandwiches from the bar menu.

"So, where are you girls from?"   Joan says,

"We're from Toledo, Ohio, just visiting New York for the first time."

"I'm from Connecticut, I'm an architect. I just came down on the train to meet a possible date that didn't work out."

I don't tell them that I had been answering personal ads in the magazine.

"So, where are you staying in the city?" Phyllis says,

" We have a hotel room up on 42$^{nd}$ street. We walked all the way down here."

"So did I, it's a beautiful evening in New York, great weather to stroll and check out the city sights."

After we schmooze for an hour over our sandwiches and another drink, I say,

"So, shall we head out?", and we all leave together and head back uptown. As we're strolling up the street arm in arm, some guy says to me,

"What's this with having **two** girls? Why can't you share the wealth?"

I just give him a resigned smile and keep going.

We stop in at a T-shirt store and are amazed at the different messages on them. We talk to the proprietor and learn that you can order whatever message and/or image that you want, and wait 15 minutes or so and it will be made to order for you. Phyllis and Joan start giggling about possible horny messages they could get and start laughing about howtheir husbands will react when they get back to Toledo.  I say,

" Oh go ahead, get what you want, that's what coming to New York City is all about."

Joan considers one where two girls are talking and one says,

"It's hard to be good", and her friend  with big almost exposed tits is pounding on a surface and saying,

"It's got to be hard to be good."

I say,

"Oh go ahead and get that one, your husband will love it."

So Joan goes up to the cashier and sheepishly places the order.

In the meantime, Phyllis has found one where a guy is talking to a girl whose mouth has a dour, negative expression while her eyes are mischievously sparkling, and the guy is saying

"Your lips are saying no, no, but there's Yes, Yes in your eyes."  She says to me,

"What do you think?" and I tell her,

"Yes, Yes, that's one of my favorite expressions. I also think your husband will also love that one."

So she orders it. In the meantime, I have ordered a tee shirt where a guy is watching concrete run down a chute while saying,

"I (image of a big red heart) concrete."

As we are leaving the store, I say,

"So, what's next?", and Joan says,

"Why don't you come up to our room for a night cap. We've got a nice bottle of Courvoisier up there."

"Terrific, that's one of my favorite ways to conclude a day."

On we go up to their 42$^{nd}$ Street hotel hand-In-hand.

Almost from the moment we enter their room, I am kissing Joan while Phyllis is hugging me from behind and caressing my hair. After a few minutes of heavy kissing with entwined tongues, I turn around and kiss Phyllis just as intently, while Joan caresses me from behind. While Phyllis and I continue with the kissing, Joan goes to get the cognac and pours three generous snifters.

While the three of us are enjoying the cognac, I am little by little removing their clothing as well as my own. As I am feeling that we are headed for a full-blown three-way, curiously enough things go into some kind of holding pattern when we get to the stage of wearing only underwear. Joan seems to disappear somewhere while I am wearing only Jockey shorts which are tented by my erection. I am kissing Phyllis while we are lying together on the big king-sized bed but Joan has gone somewhere over on the other side of the bed and is not in contact with us.

It seems as though these girls are shy in front of one another. In trying to make progress getting the rest of Phyllis' clothes off, I am confronted by such heavily armored undergarments that I may as well be in bed with an Armadillo, and she is making no effort to help me. It's as though the symphony gradually groans to a halt from a lot of wild sounds winding down to silence. Clearly these girls have no appetite for no-holds barred three-way sex. Phyllis stops kissing me or engaging with me in any way, so I put my clothes back on and say goodbye. Neither of the girls ever utters another word.

While waiting for the wedding with Cynthia in Riverdale, I answer a couple of more ads. One reads,

"**Attractive Professional Woman**- Warm, loves animals, has 11-yr. old daughter, 5'8", 45. Seeks bright, professional, huggable man. Forever." Another reads:

"**Stamford, CT**- Very pretty, sincere, slim Jewish widow, 46, seeks special man to share her life. Note/photo please." The third one really catches my eye,

"**Single Black Female**, High-ranking corporate executive, 40's, statuesque, linear and lovely, seeks intelligent, energetic male, who, like me, enjoys life and a good laugh. Willingness to explore new experiences a must. Photo/note."

Remembering that very attractive black woman with my mother that evening long ago, I enthusiastically answer that one first, thinking that meeting a beautiful black woman could prove to be a game-changer. I am thrilled to get a response from her only three days after mailing my note and photo to her. Her name is June, and we agree to meet that next weekend at the fountain at Lincoln Center, or so I think.

The following Saturday afternoon, at 5 p.m., I am strolling around the fountain at Lincoln Center, anticipating seeing a statuesque black beauty, which never occurs. I stay there till 5:30 before giving up. I see plenty of women there, but none of them are black, statuesque and alone. The next day, I write to June again and ask her why she never showed. She responds on the next mail and says that she thought we were meeting at Rockefeller Center, and that she is not familiar with Lincoln Center.

With that, my dream of meeting and romancing a lovely black lady evaporates. I wonder how a corporate executive, no matter how statuesque, can be ignorant of Lincoln Center. I never do understand what fountain in Rockefeller Center she thought we were meeting at, but I console myself with the thought that perhaps she is too tall for me anyway. I look back at her ad and see that she had never mentioned how tall she was.

The warm, attractive professional woman who loves animals turns out to be of no interest to me, but I meet the Stamford, Ct, woman at the Lincoln Center fountain three nights later. Corinne is a slim, pretty woman just like her ad said, and is also a petite brunette, just my type.

We have fun, open conversation from the get-go, and also go across the street to Oneal's for a drink and snacks. After only one martini, we even begin to kiss at the bar. I realize that this relationship could get physical in a hurry. I suggest that we go down to the village to have dinner at the Minetta Tavern, which I am familiar with because of going there with Sheila when we had gone to foreign films at the Angelika that never seemed to make it up to Connecticut.

The Minetta is a great, informal, arty low-key restaurant, but I'm embarrassed to report that Corinne and I behave badly while we are there, because we do almost more hugging and kissing while we are at our table than we do eating. I never like to see other couples making out like exhibitionists in public places and here Corinne and I are doing exactly that. I'm surprised that no one in charge tells us to stop or throws us out of the place. Had we had somewhere to bed down right then and there we surely would have done so, but I don't want to spring for the cost of a New York City hotel room.

Driving her back to Grand Central to put her on a train home enables us to cool off a little, and I expect that the next time we meet will either be at my condo or at her place in Stamford when we can really find out how well we fit together, but, although we discuss both of those possibilities, we leave it vague and don't set a date or venue for our next meeting.

Even though answering women's ads has already netted me two hot dates- Cynthia and Corinne, actually three, counting Paula, in only a couple of weeks, it now occurs to me to see what will happen if I put in my own ad. This would mean that the initial information about possible women would be much more complete, since their mailed notes in response to my ad would be much more informative than the magazine ads. This would be like the plethora of letters Sam Baldwin gets in Sleepless in Seattle.

It is fun to compose the ad and also it gives me, the writer, the illusion of being in control of the situation. So I compose my own ad having in mind what Cynthia said to me after just one conversation- that she had never had a conversation like that with a man in her whole life. I am also mindful of what a number of different married women have said to me at cocktail parties over the years, that their husbands never talk with them about matters that interest them personally, and especially that their husbands don't listen to them. So I compose the following ad:

"Tired of handsome empty shells that never talk with you about who you are or what you care about? Wouldn't you like to meet a handsome, sensitive, romantic, physically-fit man who loves to dance and who actually wants to really know you and, not just do fun things together, but to share intimate conversations about what matters to you?"

The ad is a great success. I get three or four dozen responses, including a number of three, four or five page letters with photographs, and personal histories and even some video cassettes containing the same. A couple of different women send photos of themselves on the ski slopes. The range of class and education in the responding women is truly impressive in scope.

Just from the quality of the paper and the pictures, I can tell that some of the women are from working class families and some are from money and high education. Just from the poses and the clothes worn I can tell the ones with class. They have all different ethnicities, hair color and occupations.

The responders have names including Norma, Jean, Marcia, Susan, Elsa, June, Barbara, Bernice, Lennie ( not clearly a woman's name, but evidently it is in parts of South America), Dolores, Olive, Despina, Audrey, Georgea, Christa,

Natalie, Jane, Flora, Pat, Sherry, Patti, Roberta, Maureen, Daina, Rosemarie, Mary Louise and many more. They have occupations including interior designer, art curator, pianist, banker, real estate professional, aerobic dancer, clothes designer, or film producer, and some are well-off enough not to have to work.

I have a hard time deciding which letters to respond to. Some captivate me with just their wit. One woman says that clearly I am gifted, even if only with creating the hyperbole contained in my ad. That one almost gets me just because of the sharp tongue. As a result of responding to the letters I get, I start spending most of my spare time running around the New York Metropolitan area with different women.

I meet one woman with an obvious upper-crust background in her apartment high above Riverside Drive. Maybe I am put off by that background, which I do not share, but what I feel is that this woman is a decade older than I am. She may not be that much older in physical years, but her body language makes me think so. Ironically, although we are alone in her apartment, there is no possibility of a movement toward the bedroom, whereas Corinne and I at the Minetta Tavern would have made rapid and full use of the bedroom in this upper class spread since at the Minetta we were half-way to the bedroom before we even left the table.

By contrast, I meet a woman in a diner in Fort Lee in Jersey who has gone to a state university with whom I have a very unsatisfactory meeting because she thinks I am dissing her education and background based on the fact that I went to Yale. I spend a different evening with an attractive brunette woman probably in her fifties in Ridgewood, New Jersey. After a meal and drinks at an Italian restaurant near her apartment, we go there for a nightcap. She is showing me a book of photographs of naked native people in Africa taken by Leni Reifenstahl, the famous maker of the 1930's puff piece about Hitler and the Nazis- "Triumph of the Will".

We are sitting next to each other on the couch as she shows me the book, and all it takes is for me to turn and look at her before we are kissing deeply and she is complaining,

" I never should have let this happen. I had no intention of letting things go so far so fast."

I try to make her feel better, but the romantic mood is broken by her having revealed what amounts to desperation to be intimate with a man once again, obviously after a long hiatus.

Speaking of the upper crust, I meet a woman from real wealth named Louise who lives in Rye, New York. I meet her at a restaurant in Litchfield, CT, with which she is familiar from having gone to summer concerts at Tanglewood.

Over lunch, I am telling her about my matriculation at Yale

School of Architecture, and about concerts at Tanglewood that I have attended.

"The most memorable event for me at Tanglewood", I tell her, "is when my wife and I were there with friends to see Mstislav Rostropovich play Dvorak's chello concerto.- that was special!"

Louise says,

"Yes, I know what you mean, the most memorable concerts are when you see some specially gifted performer. " I say,

"Yes, the power of certain classical works can be greatly magnified by the performers. I especially enjoy works that are conducted by Carlos Kleiber, because of the interpretation he brings to the music. I have recordings of La Traviata and Beethoven's 5$^{th}$ symphony which he conducts with such a thrillingly brisk pace that it brings the music to vibrant life."

Louise is ecstatic at my reference to Carlos Kleiber, whom she has seen conduct on special occasions in the past, some of which were in Europe. In her experience, most people don't have any idea who Carlos Kleiber is, and the fact that I not only know who he is but especially like his work puts me in a very high position in her estimation.

From this I intuit that she may have had some serious disappointments in trying to meet men at her stage in life who can match up to her own experience, education level and cultural level and therefore to her expectations of those things in any new relationship.

At the conclusion of our lunch in Litchfield, Louise and I make arrangements to meet in New Haven to see an art film, which we do, without significant event- following which we meet for another movie in Stamford.  I am definitely proceeding with care and caution with Louise.  We haven't even kissed after three dates.  I'm not even sure what's in it for me, I'm simply going with the flow.

Pretty soon the flow leads to an invitation from Louise to accompany her to a formal dance at a ballroom on an upper floor of the Park Plaza Hotel on 59th street.  At that event I feel like a stranger in paradise.  I've never before attended any event with such a large number of wealthy people.  Of course I'm wearing a tux, which I've only worn before at weddings or proms.

Louise and I are sitting at a table with about a dozen stuffy people, none of whom I have ever met or even seen, including one large guy whom I have never heard of who is evidently an opera singer.  At one point Louise introduces me to Jerzy Kosinski, author of "The Painted Bird", who is making the rounds of the crowd, and who is going to commit suicide a year later.  I do a few dances with Louise to an orchestra which sounds a lot like Guy Lombardo, and these are awkward dances. She is nowhere near as good a dancer as Sheila, and I have to work hard to make sure that she is staying with me on the dance floor. All in all, this dance party is a very surreal experience, seeming like something happening to someone else fifty years ago in some foreign place like Prague or Budapest.

The only thing comparable to it in my experience, but of a far different quality, is when Sheila and I begin our opera experience by seeing Rigoletto at the old Met at 1411 Broadway, just two years before the building is demolished. The character of that building and its furnishings make one feel like one is in Europe. I am especially impressed that the reverberations of the music can be clearly felt in the seating and the structure of the floor.

The fact that a single singer can stand at the front of the stage with an entire symphony orchestra playing behind the singer and have his or her voice clearly heard over the orchestra is astounding. It takes me a number of years of opera-going at the new Met at Lincoln Center before I get used to the new house and forget the old one.

My adventure with Louise only finally ends a couple of weeks later when she at long last invites me to her home in Rye. Her home is a mansion of a type familiar to me from having visited Sheila's rich relatives' homes in Minnesota and Pittsburgh. The large dining room with only the two of us seated at the table full of place settings and finger bowls, andwith huge tapestries on the walls with a fox-hunting theme is evocative of those distant relatives of my wife.

But our relationship finally comes to an end, not because I am awkward with the extra silverware and the finger bowls, or because of the complete disparity in our lifestyles, but for the simple reason that Louise doesn't have the faintest idea how to kiss. After dinner, while sitting together on the couch, with no one else in the house but Louise's housekeeper in some distant room, when our mouths at last come together, all I get is teeth. I may as well be trying to make love to a wild animal who is looking at me more as a meal than a lover.

We rather quickly part, I leave in my car to drive back to reality, and that is the end of that. My going through the motions comes to an end then and there.. On the way home I ask myself, Who was I kidding- what in God's name did I think I was doing? It was like I was in training to be a con man, but I was not gaining anything from it.

When the day of the Riverdale wedding arrives, I get another slice of unfamiliar life, but at least this one has a connection to a part of my own family. By this time I have begun sleeping with Cynthia. The first time is at her apartment in New Rochelle when I am on the way home from the Catskills where I have visited my other new girlfriend who I will tell you about in a few pages.

I stop in at Cynthia's place in the evening, and we get into bed very shortly after listening to Tchaikovsky's violin concerto, one of my favorites, over a couple of drinks. The sex is OK, nothing to write home about, but it includes oral as well as genital. The next morning I mention to Cynthia that I don't have a toothbrush. She laughs as she lends me hers, quoting Gloria Radner's comment about how ridiculous it is for couples to worry about the sanitation problem of using the other's toothbrush after their mouths have been in every opening in their lover's bodies.

Another time after she has stayed overnight at my condo, there is a minor embarrassment when my condo neighbors, who have also been friends and customers, stop into my unit to find Cynthia's brassiere conspicuously draped over a chair in the dining room. It's really no problem because no one is under any illusions about the nature of my relationship with Cynthia.

The wedding ritual at the Riverdale synagogue is not completely different from any wedding I have ever attended, this being a reform congregation, but the one different thing is that there are a number of men participating in the ceremony who are wearing dark clothes and hats with extremely wide brims. To me it is very strange to have men wearing large-brimmed hats indoors. The fact that my mother is from a Jewish family provides no help in understanding what is going on this day in Riverdale.

I had never been to any Jewish ceremony connected with her family. In fact, the only wedding I ever attend with the Jewish part of my own family is in a Catholic Church in New Jersey- (everything interesting in my life seems to be connected to Jersey!) On that occasion, the son of my cousin, who is in turn the son of one of my mother's brothers, after having, because of attaining the age of thirteen and having his Bar Mitzvah, brought his whole immediate family back into the Jewish fold after they had spent many years blending in with their Catholic neighbors- even having a Christmas tree in their living room- is now marrying a shicksa, a pretty curly- haired blonde Catholic girl.

I am sitting in the sanctuary waiting for the service to begin and trying to calm down my Aunt Rosa, who is the bridegroom's grandmother, and who is almost freaking out because she is sitting facing a life-sized crucifix at the front of the church which carries a large sculptured likeness of the crucified Christ. Evidently I am successful because she continues to sit there right up until the priest powerfully intones at the climax of the service:

" What the lord has put together, let no man put asunder,"

which is one of the few things that typically happens in a church that truly gives me a thrill.

Even though we have been living apart for several months, I still go on dates with Sheila, believe it or not, even taking her to New York.  We have always loved going out to dinner and to art films or the opera together, and we continue to do so, despite not sleeping together at the moment.  She is very glad to hear my voice when I call her up to ask her out.  As a couple who have been married for several decades, there is something exciting and refreshing about going out on dates, almost like a return to the spontaneity before we were married.

After a decade of being regular season ticket holders at the Met, we have now moved up to enjoy possession of a pair of great family-circle seats which are in the center near the front of the section, close to the front but back a couple of rows so that our vision and concentration is never broken by people passing in the aisle in front of the family circle.  These family circle seats are great because they are inexpensive, yet affording the same elevated panoramic view of the stage afforded by seats in the balcony or the dress circle, although of course not comparable to the great seats in the front of the grand tier, which Sheila and I have enjoyed in the past in the form of gift seats from one of her employers or one of my clients.

We are in the city to see Il Trovatore, and are having dinner at the Ginger Man, of course with a drink first.  I always have a gin martini, but Sheila has a Dubonnet, an aperitif wine.  It's ironic that I drink much more heavily than she does, because, before we got married, my mother worried that I was hooking up with a family full of alcoholics and divorcees, whereas now I'm the one who is drinking and running around with other women than my wife.

Sheila asks me,

"So what are you doing with other women?"

"I answered some personal ads in New York Magazine so I've been dating a few women in the New York City area. I'm having a lot of fun, but there is nothing serious."

"What about Marion?"

"I haven't seen her (which is a lie). She is living with some guy in her New Haven apartment."

"I'm still very much afraid of her. I don't trust her any farther than I can throw her, and I don't trust **you** with her either."

I don't mention to Sheila that in fact I have seen Marion a few times without getting into bed with her, although we have passionately kissed in the car. I have not been able to get Marion completely out of my mind, so Sheila is right not to trust me with Marion.

"What about the psychiatrist, are you seeing someone?"

"I haven't found one yet, but I'm working on it."

"When are you going to get your act together and find out

about yourself?"

I try to assure her that I will get going on that, but I'm probably not very convincing.

We go across the street to the Met. I enjoy being in the crowd there crossing Broadway, because I feel like I am really in the center of society in this city. We see a fantastic production of Il Trovatore, with Pavarotti, Marilyn Horne and Joan Sutherland, three of the greatest in a single opera. I'm thinking that even Louise would be impressed by this cast.

It is remarkable that I can talk freely with Sheila about all of these women that I am dating. Sheila is correctly unworried about them, she seems to know me better than I know myself. As long as it is not Marion, she can abide my running around and she seems quietly confident that before too long, I will get it out of my system. She just wants me to get going talking to a psychiatrist so that I can become more content with myself and thereby be more comfortable in my own skin without needing to be adored by women.

I get a letter from a woman answering my ad named Carolyn who designs hats for women, and who always wears one herself. When I meet her at the Lincoln center fountain, she is wearing a colorful chapeau and flashes me a grin from ear to ear when she sees me approaching.

"You must be Carolyn, I'm Grady."

"Yes, how did you know?, she asks sarcastically."

I follow my usual dating routine and take her across the street to the bar at O'Neal's where we enjoy a scintillating conversation about everything under the sun. She is Jewish and a liberal democrat. Her marriage ended when she began an affair with an old friend from college. She makes it clear that her affair with this guy involved a lot of heavy sex which she enjoyed immensely.

This is a bit intimidating because I had never considered myself to be a great swordsman in bed, but I persist with her because we have so much in common, including a love of opera, and we are getting along famously. We clearly like each other and enjoy each other's company, so I say,

"Would you like to go to the Met with me? I still have two great seats in the front area of the family circle where you can see and hear everything and are undisturbed by people moving around in that part of the theater."

"Sure, I'd love it", says Carolyn, so I agree to notify her soon of a couple of possible performances.

Three weeks later we are sitting in d3 and d5 enjoying a matinee performance of Masked Ball. After the king dies, we walk up Broadway to Carmen's restaurant. On the way we happen to bump into Carolyn's niece Frances and a friend who are also walking on Broadway. We have a brief conversation about nothing at all, during which the girls seem pretty excited about something.

After we have a delicious cheese lasagna and some red wine at Carmen's, Carolyn invites me up to her apartment in the 80's on the upper West side. She sits me down on the sofa with another glass of red wine and then goes into another room to check her answering machine. Carolyn must not realize that I can hear the machine but I do hear a very excited female voice exclaiming,

"Aunt Carolyn, where did you find such a beautiful man? I can't believe that I saw you with someone so gorgeous! Gloria and I would love to find one from the same place you got him!"

Carolyn comes back into the living room without saying anything and I don't let on that I heard the answering machine message, but we right away begin to do some deep kissing, while she is murmuring "um, um". We enjoy this for quite a few minutes, but neither of us makes any motions toward removing any clothing or heading for the bedroom. Carolyn tells me,

"I haven't mentioned that I own a home upstate in the Catskills. Do you think you might like to come up there for a weekend? I can actually use your expertise on some structural problems with the house. It must be at least 40 years old."

"Sure, I'd love to come up.  Just let me know when is a good time."

"I'll call you in a few days when I can see my schedule clearly."

A few days later we talk on the phone and arrange for me to drive up to a place called "Fleischmann's" on Route 28.  She explains how to find her house, and  I have no problem finding it.  It turns out to be a pretty large, rambling three or four-bedroom vacation home with a screened porch and a very large open deck.  The décor of the interior is from between the wars and the place has a good deal of charm as a summer cottage.

After a meal she prepares, and some watching tennis on TV, we get into bed for the first time.  We are warm and cuddly together and it feels very nice to be inside her, but we are pretty restrained this first time.  Nevertheless, we sleep in the same bed despite there being many beds and bedrooms in the house.  The next morning after breakfast, Carolyn shows me some of the problems with the house.  The first thing she shows me is the deck, which is sagging.  An inspection of the underside of the deck, which is fortunately five or six feet above ground so it is easy to walk around underneath and evaluate the situation, exhibits a fair amount of rotting in the 2 x 10 floor joists. I tell her,

"Carolyn, your deck is in danger of collapsing if you don't replace some of these joists that have rotted. I can do the work myself, if you order in the necessary materials."

"I can do that, but you'll have to give me the list of materials you will need. In fact, we can go down to the lumber yard together and place the order once you have it prepared."

So I spend the rest of the morning assembling a list of materials, including a large number of 12 ft. pressure-treated 2 x 10's. Carolyn says,

"We can get the materials ordered for delivery on another weekend when you can come up here. This afternoon I'd like you to accompany me to a neighborhood party to celebrate my friend's daughter's engagement."

The party seems to consist mostly of Jews in their 40's and 50's, so Carolyn and I are both in an appropriate age range, and I'm even compatible ethnically, but Carolyn never accepts that, and she's probably right. I don't feel that I am Jewish to the extent of feeling as though I'm really one of them and Carolyn's attitude reinforces that alienation. I enjoy the humor of Borsht Belt comics like Jackie Mason, but Carolyn says that I am not qualified to truly understand the humor. Evidently being Jewish has more to do with experience and upbringing than it does with bloodlines.

Nevertheless, Carolyn makes sure to introduce me to all of her friends so I gather that she is showing me off. The party is on a Sunday afternoon in the late afternoon, so afterwards I head home, except that, as I said earlier, I stop off in New Rochelle to see Cynthia.

My running around with women in the New York City area continues for a couple of more months, although it is now confined to Cynthia and Carolyn. I get into bed with them both a few more times, which does not lead to any intensifying of feelings. The thing with Cynthia ends when she is at my condo complaining that I continue to see Carolyn. I make no effort to hide one from the other, so it is right out on the table to be reacted to, which is what Cynthia does, and she is not wrong. She wants a man to herself, as I believe all women do, so I am not surprised or even hurt when she finally drives away, never to return. Cynthia thinks the problem is Carolyn; she never learns that in fact I am still married to Sheila.

I continue to see Carolyn both in the city and upstate and she doesn't know about Sheila either. I generally drive my car down to the upper west side, but parking near Carolyn's apartment is much more dangerous than parking in Lincoln Center. One night when I have my car there, we drive down Fifth Avenue with the convertible top down on a warm summer night and are able to make the entire trip for fifty blocks without stopping at a single red light. On nights like that, I can feel rich as Rockefeller even though I hardly have a pot to piss in, since I have been blowing all of my spare money on careening around the city with other women.

When I am up at Fleischmann's, I feel much more domesticated since I am staying with a woman in her own home, but eventually I begin to chafe at providing all the free labor. I start to think this is just history repeating itself, it is an echo of my father working for Mi-hih-nih-hih, and for the same payback, just the affection of another woman.

In point of fact, if I look at the situation with clear eyes, I realize that I am not running around with all these women because I really need to, I am only doing it because I can, because the women all find me attractive. The thing that is really casting a shadow over Sheila and me is my desire for Marion, the precise thing that Sheila is actually worried about. I have known Marion for years and she has intrigued me for years. There is a solid base there that is lacking with all of these other women that I have only known recently.

The thing is that now, just in the time that I have stayed away from Marion, she has realized the strength of my tie with Sheila, despite her speech about Sheila not owning me. She is smart enough to realize that Sheila really does own my heart and that actually being able to get me away from Sheila is a doubtful stretch, so she has now taken up with an older local businessman who seems to provide her with a realistic possibility of long-term support, and she doesn't want to jeopardize that possibility by too seriously continuing to mess around with me.

Although my realization about my father and Mi-hih-nih-hih has ended my adventure with Carolyn, now I have a new problem. I learn that one of my unfinished and unsold condo units has a potential buyer. Beverly Thomas is a divorced woman from North Carolina who has relocated to Connecticut and is interested in unit 34. My realtor introduces her to me at the unit and I see that she is a beautiful, sexy, stacked woman in her 40's with bedroom eyes. Oh, oh, here I go again, but it may be OK because she also has a boyfriend.

We make the deal and arrange for her to move into the bedroom while temporarily storing her living room and dining room furniture while we finish the living spaces. It is warm weather, so after she has already moved her bed into the unit and is sleeping there, I am out in front of the condo with my shirt off working on installation of the water meter underground by the curb.

This has now become a familiar sequence, and soon after that day with the water meter, I am in the unit discussing finish flooring with Beverly and she has become very flirtatious. She says, "Why don't you join me with a chicken sandwich and a glass of wine?", so I do. What's not to like? Here I am with a gorgeous well-built sexy woman who is coming on to me in her own condo, and who is spectacularly available with a comfortable bed only a few steps away from where we are starting to flirt. As we embrace, I am hard as a rock, but, surprisingly, as we begin to kiss, it all goes away and my member betrays me as I completely lose my erection. My body does not want to do this, and our incipient coitus fails to happen. In the event it is quite embarrassing and I apologize to Beverly that evidently I am not ready to get involved.

Actually, I am just finally wising up to the reality that Dr. Rubens later points out to me. After I have described being with a woman who wants me in her bed, Dr. Rubens points out the obvious truth when he says, "After all, Grady, you don't **have** to go to bed with her!"

After that we are able to complete the construction and the contract and go our separate ways. I even meet her boyfriend one day while working on the living room flooring. He acts suspicious around me but nothing overt happens. Two months after completing the sale, I happen to be just down the street from Beverly's unit one day talking with another potential buyer who may be interested in one of the waterfront units if we can agree on some substantial improvements. As we are standing on the sidewalk talking, I notice out of the corner of my eye that Beverly's boyfriend is out in front of her unit washing his car. Just as I notice him, he notices me, and, much to my amazement, he starts to stride purposefully toward me with fire in his eye. In an instant I realize what must have happened.  Beverly must have suggested to him that she cuckolded him with me and he is storming over in my direction with the intention of beating me up or at least landing a few haymakers.  I have the presence of mind to do nothing and to act like I haven't even noticed that he is heading over toward me.  I turn back to talk with the people I am meeting and pretend that nothing untoward is happening.

Sure enough, he never comes over to us and in a furtive later glance I see that he has returned to his car washing.  I deduce from this that he must have thought he was completely mistaken and that whatever Beverly had told him was just some lie to get under his skin.  In this moment I am grateful to my cock for seeming to have a mind of its own in realizing the danger of getting involved with Beverly.  With my penis, discretion turns out to be the better part of valor.  I have a smart cock, not the dumb tool automatically popping up out of the mud that Jimmie Mansfield had all those decades ago at the boys' club summer camp.

This episode with Beverly tells me that I better get going talking with a psychiatrist so that I can get as smart as my cock, and maybe I can even get Sheila to take me back and I can end all this nonsense with other women.

# CHAPTER 5

## KNOW THYSELF

I contact our regular family physician, explain that I need some hopefully brief psychiatric counseling, and ask for a recommendation. My physician recommends Dr. Rubens, who has an office in New Haven near Yale. I meet Dr. Rubens a week later and like him right away, although his fee of $300 per hour seems pretty steep to me. Still, I accept it without quibble because I hope to be able to sort myself out in only a few sessions. I make arrangements for a ten o'clock hour every Tuesday morning.

The following Tuesday, I arrive and am welcomed into Dr. Rubens' private office. We sit in comfortable chairs at right angles to one another. The room also features a fireplace with dental molding which is probably not actually used, a couch with end tables along the other wall opposite the two chairs we are sitting in, and a writing desk where I presume Dr. Rubens makes notes and does his correspondence. The décor is evidently designed to make patients feel that they are in their own living rooms so that they will feel comfortable and relaxed.

After some preliminaries, in which I inform him about my education, my work and my marriage, Dr. Rubens asks me,

"So, what is on your mind?" I say, "I've gotten involved in an affair with another woman, whose name is Marion. She is one of our social friends and I've been in bed with her a couple of times."

Dr. Rubens asks,

"Is this Marion the only woman you've been with other than Sheila?"

"No, there have been many others. The funny thing is that I seem to get into sexual situations without really intending to do so."

Dr. Rubens perks up at this statement.

"That sounds very interesting. Tell me about how these situations happen." I say,

"The first one that comes to mind is this client who exposed herself to me seemingly out of the blue."

I proceed to tell Dr. Rubens about Barb Rusk.

"When I got to the front door to look at her brochure on doors, I couldn't believe what I was looking at. Here she was in a see-through blouse with her large boobs right in front of my face and I had to gulp and pretend I wasn't seeing what I was seeing. I was somehow able to ignore the provocation and just proceed with our legitimate business."

Dr. Rubens asks, " What do you think provoked that display?" "The only thing I can think of is that, a few weeks earlier, I had been driving around with her looking at front entries on other houses, and it was a very hot day, so I took off my shirt while we were driving around. Maybe this was just a case of tit for tat, no pun intended. Could it just be that since I had shown her my chest, she determined to do the same?"

Dr. Rubens says,

"That's a bit oversimplified, but one thing is clear, and that is she found your body very attractive."

"I guess she did", I say, "and that reminds me of something Marion said to me while we were in the shower together after our first time having sex. She asked me, "Are you for real?"'
Dr. Rubens asks,

"Did you ask her what she meant?"

"No, I didn't".

"Perhaps you didn't want to know", says the Doctor. "This is a very interesting beginning, but our time is up. I'll see you next Tuesday morning."

In the car afterwards, I wonder about that last question I talked about with Dr. Rubens. Why didn't I ask Marion what she meant? Do I not want to know the truth about myself? I remember that our social friend Gen had said to me, when we got into the altogether,

"You don't know what you have."

I had never asked Gen what she meant by that statement

either.

The next week passes very slowly for me, because I am looking forward to seeing Dr. Rubens again the following Tuesday, and I have no contact with Marion. That Tuesday evening after the first session, I am out for pizza with Sheila and I inform her that I have started talking with Dr. Rubens. She is thrilled to hear it and asks me how my first session went with Dr. Rubens. I tell her,

"It was very good, we seem to relate well to each other, and I already feel a sense of some progress."

Sheila knows enough not to ask me for particulars, so she just says

"Good, let's hope that continues. Grady, why don't you come on home with me for some dessert. I made your favorite chocolate cake."

Sheila knows that I especially love chocolate cake with creamy white frosting and she has always loved dessert as the best part of any meal.

After cake, we are in the kitchen cleaning up while the radio is playing some oldies but goldies. The radio plays Louis Armstrong's version of "It was just one of those things", and the music is so danceable that we begin to dance around the kitchen. I love to hold Sheila in my arms, and I am taken back to the first time I danced with her at the service club in high school, when I was so amazed by her lightness on her feet. I also love to feel her ample breasts pressing against my chest, and of course I realize how much better a dancer she is than Louise at the Park Plaza. I rediscover that Sheila's and my bodies fit together like a couple of puzzle pieces.

The following Tuesday, it is a beautiful sunny morning, and I am happy to be going to my appointment with Dr. Rubens. Dr. Rubens starts off by asking,

"What was your first sexual experience with a girl?"

I tell him, "Other than petting to climax and blow jobs, It was at college, after I started arguing with this assertive female upper classman who was strutting around our fraternity as if she owned it. For some reason she seemed not to be put off by my criticizing her, but actually turned on. She sat on my lap, we started kissing, and then it was off to my dorm room. It was very fast, but I do remember that **she** also said something to me. She said, 'you look better and better the more clothes you take off."

"It sounds to me", said Dr. Rubens, "that she saw the same thing that Barbara Rusk saw. Evidently you have a body that is very appealing to women but you aren't very aware of it".

"I've become more aware of it in recent years."

Dr. Rubens goes on to say,

"But, of course, that could be bad news or good news."

"What do you mean?"

"This is what we need to get into", says Dr. Rubens.

"Let's take it a little bit further as we go along. But first, let's get the rest of the story about your history of sex with women other than Sheila."

I tell Dr. Rubens about Jane Hershey, Gloria Hansen and Dahlia Haverson which did not lead to actual sex, and then I begin to tell the Doctor about Gen.

"When she got naked, I saw that she was a natural blonde. But I was reluctant to have sex with her, and she definitely sensed my holding back. After we were both naked, she said to me,

'You don't know what you have.' I didn't ask her what she meant. I was not sure if she simply meant that my cock was bigger than her husband's, or something more."

"Well", says Dr. Rubens, "The pattern here is quite clear. You obviously have a body that is very appealing to women. Whenever they see you without a shirt, they come on to you, whether or not they say anything to you. Sam, Jane Hershey, Gen and Marion all said what was on their minds, but Gloria Hansen, Barbara Rusk, and Dahlia Haverson all came on to you without saying anything."

"I believe that makes me finally understand an event that happened on Cape Cod a few years ago. Sheila and I and the boys had just arrived at a new remote beach on Cape Cod when I spotted two girls in bikinis quite a way up the beach. They looked very good in their bikinis with very ample cleavages and I looked up the beach at them for a few seconds, during which they were looking right back at me. Sheila and I and the boys had just begun to set up our chairs, blanket and umbrella when these girls appeared right next to us, smiling and saying Hi." Nobody said anything else and very soon they went back to where they had come from.

Sheila and I discussed our consternation at the appearance of these girls, wondering if they could be prostitutes. They didn't look a bit like whores, just very well-built young ladies in bikinis. Now, in view of these other events which seem to have a common thread, I'm beginning to see what it is."

"That's right, Grady, it wasn't only that you were looking at the girls and were impressed with their bodies. The fact is that they were looking at **your** body and were equally impressed. Evidently, they had caught sight of you up the beach at the same time as you caught sight of them, and they couldn't believe their eyes at that distance, so they just had to come up to see if you actually looked as good up close".

"With that, we'll have to stop. We will continue with this line next Tuesday, but it appears that your problem lies in the fact that, without fully realizing it, you have the body of an Adonis. This is supremely ironic because what to you is a problem is something that almost all other guys would kill for."

I leave Dr. Rubens office in a bit of a haze. I had never realized that women consistently see me as a kind of Adonis. This is a big fact to get my mind around and to come to grips with. How is this going to play out in my intense interest in Marion and in my marriage to Sheila?

During that following week, I remember a number of other odd events that now begin to make sense. When I next see Dr. Rubens, I say,

"This whole development concerning my physique is very surprising to me, but during this past week I thought of a couple of other events that seemed mysterious at the time, but now I can see begin to fit the pattern. A couple of years ago, I am riding around town on a hot summer day in my convertible with my top off, not only off the car, but also off myself. An attractive dark-haired woman comes peeling around a corner in an SUV heading toward me. When she gets close, she ostentatiously pretends to throw herself out her car door window, as though she is dropping dead."

"Right", says Dr. Rubens, "she is telling you that you are drop-dead gorgeous."

"And, just last summer, Sheila and I are relaxing on a beach blanket at the town beach and I become aware that a good-looking young woman on a nearby blanket, again in a bikini with ample cleavage, keeps staring at me. Not only that, but then I realize that she is using the popsicle she has just bought from a vendor's cart to simulate fellatio in a very obvious, unambiguous way, all while continuing to look over at me. I can't believe she is doing this right in plain sight at the town beach frequented by families."

"I also recall that, ironically, a few years ago I had decided to try to get some work modeling, since I knew I was good-looking and I could have used some supplemental income because I wasn't really making money designing and building homes, even though I got them designed and built, because all the profit got eaten up in costs. I got an appointment at a modeling agency in New York while I was in my 40's, but because I kept my hair and was in excellent physical shape, I could still pass for 30's.

The guy in charge there at the agency set me up with a photographer to take some pictures of me for a modeling portfolio to try and attract some customers who might be interested in my modeling services. The photographer took photos of me in a business suit and some with a topcoat on, and he even took one of me in work clothes using a skill saw on a board. But it never occurred to either of us to try some poses with a bathing suit or with just undershorts, because both the photographer and myself were blissfully unaware that my most outstanding, handsome physical feature Is my body, not my face!"

Dr. Rubens says, "More accurately, I would say it is the combination of your face and your body. Had you known that about yourself, you might have ended up in nothing but underwear on a huge brightly-lighted billboard over Times Square! That could certainly have changed your career path!

Calvin Klein Billboard Ad   Times Square      1991

I'm only half kidding, Grady , you never know what could have happened had this photographer gotten photos of you looking the way all of these women have seen you.  Probably you would have ended up with some lucrative jobs modeling bathing suits."

"Well", I say, "This is certainly an interesting revelation, but there is nothing I can do about it now.  I'm well into my sixties; the water has gone over the dam for a modeling career."

"Right", says Dr. Rubens, "hindsight is 20-20."

"What we have to deal with now is how you feel about Marion, Sheila and your marriage.  What actually happened that night when Sheila discovered you with Marion?"

I proceed to describe that memorable evening, including the part about Marion standing and confronting Sheila wearing nothing but panties, and telling Sheila , " But you don't **own** him!"  Dr. Rubens says, " Yes, that display of chutzpah is impressive, but I'm even more impressed by Sheila quitting her out-of-town job and coming up there to confront you and Marion.  Clearly, Sheila's a real fighter!  She wants to save her marriage, and is willing to fight hard to do so. Of course, she doesn't legally own you, but evidently she still loves you and wants to hang on to you. It's great that we are now getting down to the nitty gritty. To be continued next Tuesday."

The following Tuesday,  I begin to tell Dr. Rubens about my

moving over to the condo and making dates with women through the personal ads in New York Magazine rather than sleeping alone in the condo. After I show him the handsome photo in the snow I used to attract females in New York and tell him about several of the womens' responses and about some of the dates, I also tell him about overhearing Carolyn's answering machine. Dr. Rubens says,

" It sounds like you have been just carrying out this same pattern ad infinitum without really getting anywhere. You are not learning anything new and you don't know any more about yourself or about how you feel about Sheila and Marion than you did before. In other words, you are just spinning your wheels in the sand. Did it ever occur to you to ask what Sheila sees in you? Did she marry you, raise two sons with you and live with you all these years because she sees you as some kind of an Adonis? Why don't you think about that until we meet again next week."

Dr. Rubens' question about Sheila and me really stimulates my thinking. I remember a warm summer evening a couple of years ago when I had an epiphany about Sheila.

Sheila and I are enjoying cocktails on our screened porch when I say,

"Did you see the story about that big brouhaha at the abortion clinic in St. Louis yesterday? I can't believe that these right-to-lifers can be so rigid and outrageous in their opposition." Sheila says,

"Well, I can't defend their behavior, but I think they are right about abortion being wrong. I feel the same way myself".

I am amazed at my wife's statement.

"Yes, but what about the rights of the women that want to end their pregnancies?"

"Sure, that's another question. I don't object to what they are doing either because for them the pregnancy is something they don't want, but for me abortion is just plain wrong, because it is taking away a little life that has already begun. I could no more do that myself than fly to the moon."

I say, "Isn't it taking away potential life when a guy masturbates and sends millions of sperm cells in Kleenex into the waste basket or the toilet?

"Grady, You know perfectly well that masturbation is different because no new life has actually begun. That doesn't happen until a sperm cell swims its way into the uvula and penetrates the wall of an egg. Menstruation is actually the same thing on the female side. The woman loses lots of eggs over the years in her menstrual blood flow every month. These are not life because no sperm has made contact with any of these eggs. The millions of fish eggs that female fish lay on the river bottom don't become little fish until the male fish sprays his sperm over the eggs and some of them become fertilized and can grow into young fish.

I say, "yeah, and it's a scientific fact that no human egg can grow into new life until it is fertilized with sperm from a male. So, isn't it amazing that Jesus's disciples were able to sell that bill of goods about Joseph not being the actual father of Jesus, but that Jesus is really the son of "God".

Sheila says, "yes, but in those days people did not have the knowledge of biology that we do today, so they could accept the myth as being actually true. I say,

"Yeah, and now today we know that a virgin actually **can** give birth because the doctors have developed a way of introducing male sperm into her uterus by artificial insemination. Still, I really feel sorry for Jesus' actual father, Joseph. He is still shown as being present at the birth- he is one of the figures in the standard manger scene shown in front of Catholic churches at Christmas time- yet his fatherhood has been taken away from him. His position in the manger scene is as something like a male nurse helping at the birth. He is the ultimate cuckold- he's been cuckolded by none other than God".

"Yes", says Sheila, "he is easily as pitiable a figure as Van Gogh, who died penniless and unrecognized, and now his paintings sell for tens of millions of dollars. Joseph may not have accomplished a whole lot in his life, but the one remarkable thing he did do was to father with his wife one of the most famous people in all of human history, yet that one accomplishment has been taken away from him.  And, by calling Mary a 'virgin', they are denying that he had ever even slept with his own wife."

"No", I say, "That last part is not true, they don't deny that he slept with his wife, they just claim that the first-born was conceived when Mary was still a virgin.  They don't deny that Joseph was fucking his wife during her pregnancy, and that when he appears in the manger, he really is her husband in the full sense of the word, only that he did not father the particular child that was then being born."

"Yes, I believe this is what they believe about Joseph."

"Maybe Jesus was actually fathered by the 'milkman', in which case Joseph was cuckolded by a real man in the neighborhood.  Maybe that actually happened and was the real life basis for the myth."

In college one of the dirty limericks we were fond of repeating was:

"There once was a girl from Cape Cod, who thought all good things came from God, but it wasn't the almighty that lifted her nightie, 'twas Rodger the lodger by God."

"And", I say, "the remarkable thing is that this fantastic myth of Jesus being the son of "God" is still believed by millions of people today, even while we know as a scientific certainty that life depends on an egg being fertilized by sperm".

"Sure", says Sheila, that's the power of religious belief. People can deny the reality of human evolution, which is so thoroughly documented by the fossil record, yet they can believe other fantastic concoctions dreamed up by the founders of religions like Mormonism and Scientology which are based on nothing but one person's wild fantasies."

I say, "I guess we can be thankful that at least you and I are not burdened by these impossible theories".

"Don't be so smug, Grade, I can still believe that abortion is wrong.  What is right and wrong does not depend on scientific knowledge- it is still wrong to deliberately kill a human being."

"But", I say, "We deliberately kill plenty of human beings in wartime while trying to protect our country, and when we execute convicted violent criminals."

"But Grade", "I'm not so sure that last example is right, either."

We continue with this conversation through several drinks, talking about things like women who become pregnant by being raped, and after I become more and more frustrated with my inability to logically convince Sheila of my position, I finally have a true epiphany.  I realize that not all of Sheila's positions are based on logic, but rather that many of them, including this one we are now talking about,  are based on the feeling in her stomach.  If a person feels in his or her stomach that something is not right, there is absolutely no point in arguing - the argument is fruitless because the person's position is not based on logic.  It is not based on thinking at all but on pure feeling.  Once I realize this, I relax into the unlimited love of my wife that I have felt for most of my entire life, and I am happy with the knowledge that I now know her even better than I had before.

The following week with Dr. Rubens, I tell him about this basic realization about Sheila that I had several years before, and I review my whole history with Sheila.

"I can't really say that she ever gave me the feeling that I was any kind of Adonis.  We just liked each other in every way, including our conversations.  We both found each other physically attractive and we were extremely intimate physically in every possible way."

I told Dr. Rubens about the thing Gloria Radner said that Cynthia and I laughed about and said, "The remarkable thing is that Sheila is particular about not sharing toothbrushes despite where our mouths have been on each other's bodies."

Dr. Rubens chuckled about this also.

"That bears out what you discovered about Sheila's

attitudes coming from feelings rather than always being based on logical thinking. Grady, I think that our sessions are about over. I think you are now focusing on what makes your marriage with Sheila so strong. It has nothing to do with you being an Adonis. Furthermore, the fact that women see you as an Adonis once you take your shirt off doesn't add anything to your experience with these women, as you have seen over and over. If you feel the need for further conversations in the future, don't hesitate to give me a call, but I think for now we are finished."

We part company warmly and I express my gratitude for his services and all of his help.

Coincidentally, I learn around this time that Marion has gotten married to the rich businessman and has moved to Florida, so that ends that threat, despite the fact that she has married for money and not for love. The successful conclusion of my therapy plus Marion's marriage enables me to move back home with Sheila, and we are as before, but without all the other women.

The first time in bed with her, we have a wonderful time, intimately cuddling together and enjoying each other's bodies as we have done since we were both teenagers. Sheila says,

"See, Grady, Gen was wrong, you do know what you have, you have me!"

I say, "Yeah", channeling Sony & Cher, "I've got you, babe!"

"Yes, and I've got you, you're for real and you are gorgeous!"

## EPILOGUE, TWENTY FIVE YEARS LATER

Sheila says to her daughter-in-law Ellie,

"Grady and I would love you to take our official photo for our 60th wedding anniversary.  You have taken such excellent photos of your family over the years."

"OK, I'll be happy to take it.  But I won't be able to make you look like Richard and Elizabeth.  The best I can do is to faithfully reveal how healthy and happy you two are for octogenarians."

"Great", says Grady, "at least we will look pretty cute for our age."

www.ingramcontent.com/pod-product-compliance
Lightning Source LLC
Chambersburg PA
CBHW070107290526
45789CB00005B/1953